ATTITUDE
IS
EVERYTHING

ATTITUDE IS EVERYTHING

*Nothing can stop the man
with the right mental attitude
from achieving his goal.
Nothing on earth can help the man
with the wrong attitude.*

— Thomas Jefferson

Attitude is Everything
Change Your Attitude... and You Change Your Life!

By Jeff Keller

Printed in the United States of America
First Edition, May 1999
Second Edition, January 2007

ISBN 1-891279-21-1

Published by INTI Publishing
Tampa, FL

DEDICATION ————————————————

This book is dedicated to my wife, Dolores,
for believing in me and encouraging me
to follow my dreams.

ACKNOWLEDGMENTS _____

To God, for your loving guidance and for the many blessings you have bestowed upon me.

To my mother and father, Freda and Leo Keller, for your love and support, and for the code of ethics you taught me, which has served me so well in my life.

To my brother, Marc Keller, for your enthusiastic support of my work.

To Steve Price, Katherine Glover and the entire staff at INTI Publishing for your professionalism, talent and invaluable assistance in the preparation of this book. I never imagined that doing this much work could be so much fun!

To my friend, Jim Donovan, for introducing me to INTI Publishing, and for your encouragement and guidance.

To Kathleen Regan, for designing the attractive *Attitude is Everything* logo.

To the members of the National Speakers Association, who have given so generously of their knowledge and experience, and who have helped me to develop my skills as a speaker and writer.

To all of the clients of my company, Attitude is Everything, Inc., for your business and your tremendous encouragement over the years. All of you are like family to me.

CONTENTS _____

INTRODUCTION

The Night That Changed My Life

> *The greatest discovery of my generation is that human beings can alter their lives by altering their attitudes of mind.*
>
> —William James

In 1980, I graduated from law school and thought I'd be a lawyer for the rest of my life. After all, that's what I'd wanted to do since my early teenage years.

At first, everything went according to plan. After lots of studying that summer, I passed the Bar Examination and was admitted to practice law in New York. My personal life was also on the upswing. In early 1981, I married Dolores, a law school classmate. I was on my way to much success and happiness.

Or so I thought.

But, after practicing law for a few years, I realized I wasn't happy at all.

Sure, there were some things I liked about being a lawyer. I enjoyed helping people resolve their disputes, especially when I could save them the agony of lengthy court proceedings.

Yet, there were so many things about being an attorney that I disliked — and that just seemed to drain the life out of me. Mounds and mounds of tedious paperwork and motions to be filed. Constant delays and postponements. It was not uncommon for a trial to be postponed 10 times.

I Dreaded Going To Work

I continued to grind out the work but grew more and more dissatisfied as an attorney. I was frustrated and very depressed. To put it bluntly, I didn't like my life, and saw no way that things were going to improve.

Have you ever had a job where you dreaded going to work most days — where you felt the "weight of the world" on your shoulders each day?

Well, that's how I felt. I was literally hunched over... and in pain, both physically and emotionally. I looked much older than my years. I began to get headaches all the time, and my stomach was constantly churning. Fearing that I had some serious health problem, I saw some doctors and they ordered a battery of tests. Every test came back with the same result — they couldn't find anything physically wrong with me. One of the doctors suggested that I take Maalox to calm my upset stomach.

Spiritually, I was dead. Nothing in my life had much meaning. This day-to-day drudgery was also affecting my appearance. Although I was in my late 20s, I looked like I was 40!

In the early part of 1985, shortly after I had turned 30 years old, I was burned out. And, one particular evening, while sitting alone in my den, I knew that something had to change. Not knowing what to do, I simply said out loud,

"There's got to be more to my life than this... there's got to be more than this misery and unhappiness."

Help Comes From An Unlikely Source

Later that night, I was watching TV in the den. It was around 1:00 am, and my wife, Dolores, had already gone to bed. But I was feeling so down I couldn't sleep. I "channel surfed" looking for something to occupy my time. I tuned in to, of all things, an infomercial.

Normally, I would have changed that channel in a fraction of a second, but for some reason, I listened.

The product being peddled was called *The Mental Bank* and was endorsed by actress Florence Henderson of *Brady Bunch* fame. *The Mental Bank* was a home-study course that explained how everything we achieve in life is based upon our subconscious beliefs.

> *You are not what you think you are. But what you think — YOU ARE!*
>
> — Dr. Norman Vincent Peale

I felt so desperate at that point that I decided to go for it. I pulled out my credit card and ordered the program.

That night in my den was the turning point of my life.

By the way, when I sheepishly told Dolores what I had done a day or two later, she was shocked.

"You did what?" she asked in amazement. It's not that she objected to the purchase — it was just so out of character for me to buy something like that on impulse... and worse yet, from a TV infomercial!

Several days later, *The Mental Bank* program arrived at my doorstep. And I was fascinated and excited to begin learning how our thoughts determine the quality of our lives. Prior to that time, I had never heard these ideas. Unfortunately, they don't teach you this stuff in school!

The Mental Bank program spurred me to seek out other motivational resources. I began to read books by Napoleon Hill, Og Mandino, Norman Vincent Peale and Robert Schuller. I started reading the Bible on a regular basis. And I eagerly listened to inspiring audio programs by Zig Ziglar, Earl Nightingale, Jim Rohn, Bob Proctor and many others. I felt like a person who had wandered for days in the desert with a parched throat... and then suddenly found a stream of water!

Now, I can't tell you that everything in my life changed overnight, because it didn't happen that way. But, from the moment I began to change from a negative attitude to a positive attitude, I started to get significant results.

I felt better. I had more energy. And I started to achieve goals that I would never have accomplished before… all because of a change in my attitude! I'm also happy to report that when people now ask how old I am… and I say 52, they invariably reply, "You look much younger!"

It's all in the attitude.

From Lawyer To Motivational Speaker

I continued my self-study program in my spare time, while I worked full time as a lawyer. The positive thinking was helping my attitude at work, but I felt a passion for my "hobby" that I never felt for my work, and I dreamed about the day I could walk away from my job.

In 1989, after four years of intensive research about attitude and motivational concepts, I agreed to present some adult education seminars in the evenings at a local high school. I was to be paid $30 for each two-hour class. Not the kind of money that lets you quit your day job!

> *Never underestimate your power to change yourself.*
> — H. Jackson Brown, Jr.

As I stood in front of the class to start my first seminar, I was petrified. My heart was pounding and I was sweating. But somehow I managed to muster the courage to just do it. The students loved the class, and I got a real adrenaline rush from presenting the material that had revolutionized my own life… and that had the power to do the same for others!

I was on my way.

Eventually, the speaking fees grew a little larger, and in 1990, I decided to phase out my law career over the next few years. This wasn't a simple decision. I had gone to four years of college and three years of law school to obtain my law degree. On top of that, I had spent 10 years of my life as a practicing lawyer. When you have that much invested in a career, it's not so easy to walk away.

Then, of course, there was the money issue. As a lawyer, I was on track to earn $100,000 in a few years, and I'd be earning that much — and more — for the rest of my professional career.

Taking A Stand

Although I was earning a little more income from my new "hobby," I realized that I'd have start-up expenses in launching my new enterprise. Fortunately, Dolores and I had saved some money over the years. To supplement my income, I began to sell a line of merchandise with my unique "Attitude is Everything" logo. But there was no way to avoid it — I'd have to take a huge financial step backward to start my new business... at least in the beginning.

> *A positive attitude is a person's passport to a better tomorrow.*
> *— Unknown*

And yet, it was time to move on. I felt as if I was being pulled out of the legal profession and into my new career. Whenever I spoke to an audience or wrote a motivational essay, I was so invigorated and full of life. I knew that's where I belonged.

So, I made a gradual transition — working four days a week as a lawyer, then three days a week... and then two days a week... until, in 1992, I began working full time as a motivational speaker and writer.

Trust me, my mother wasn't thrilled when I told her that I was giving up the practice of law to speak about attitude. After all, it doesn't carry the prestige of saying "My son is a lawyer!"

But these are issues you have to deal with when you take a stand in life. You have to face the fact that some people will disapprove of your decision. I also learned that you often have to let go of some things in your life and take a few steps backward before you can move forward in a new direction. Part of the price I had to pay was giving up the money, prestige and security of my legal career.

By the way, as it turned out, my mother became very supportive of my new career, especially when she saw that I was making progress — and that I really enjoyed my work.

Why am I telling you all this about my career transition? It's not to impress you with what I've done.   Believe me, I've made plenty of blunders and mistakes along the way.

I'm sharing my story because I want you to know how drastically my life changed — and how much better it got — when I made a change in my attitude.

Proof positive that, indeed, attitude is everything!

How You'll Benefit From This Book

Some final thoughts before we launch right into this material: This book can help you, no matter how positive or negative you are right now.

If you're negative, don't despair. You can use these concepts to develop and maintain a positive attitude... and to achieve incredible breakthroughs in your life.

Think, act and talk with enthusiasm and you'll attract positive results.

— Michael LeBoeuf

If you're already a positive person, you can use these principles to soar to even greater heights of success and fulfillment.

I've spent more than 20 years researching why it is that some people succeed while others achieve disappointing results. During that time, I've read a few hundred books and thousands of magazine articles on attitude and success. I've listened to more than 3,000 hours of audio cassette programs. In addition, I've interviewed countless high achievers to learn their "success secrets."

More importantly, I have personally applied each and every success strategy that is described in this book. So, I know from firsthand experience that these ideas work — and that they have the power to literally transform your life!

Please don't misunderstand me. I don't claim to be a "know-it-all" on these subjects. Far from it. I consider myself a "work in progress" and I continue to learn every day.

However, I know what it's like to have a negative attitude, because that's the kind of attitude I had for the first 30 years of my life. I know what it's like to doubt yourself and your abilities, because that's what I did for 30 years. All of the positive changes that I've made in my life are the result of practicing the principles you'll read about in this book.

Think... Speak... Act

This book is conveniently divided into three Parts, and each Part contains a series of lessons. So, if you ever need reinforcement in a particular area, it will be easy for you to turn to that lesson and re-read it.

In Part 1, *Success Begins in the Mind*, we'll be focusing on the power of attitude and belief to shape your destiny. You'll learn how your success initially depends on the way that you THINK.

In Part 2, *Watch Your Words*, we'll concentrate on the way that you SPEAK... how your attitude is reflected in your words... and how positive language can help to propel you toward your goals.

In Part 3, *Heaven Helps Those Who Act*, we'll cover the final leg of our journey. Even if you think positively... and speak positively... you won't achieve your dreams until you ACT. You can't sit back and just expect success to pay you a visit. In this section, you'll learn the action steps that will turn your dreams into reality.

When you THINK, SPEAK and ACT in ways that support your success, you're firing on all cylinders... and on the way to achieving phenomenal results in your life.

You're about to embark on a journey that will bring you success and happiness beyond your wildest dreams, so let's get started....

PART 1

Success Begins in the Mind

Success is a state of mind. If you want success, start thinking of yourself as a success.
— Dr. Joyce Brothers

LESSON 1 ─────────────

Your Attitude Is Your Window to the World

Better keep yourself clean and bright; you are
the window through which you must see the world.
— George Bernard Shaw

It was just after 1:00 pm and Sara was getting hungry. She had put in a few productive hours of work at her desk and decided to get a bite to eat at a nearby coffee shop.

A few minutes later, Sam walked into the coffee shop. He, too, was on his lunch break. Sam sat down at a table a few feet away from Sara.

The same waitress served Sara and Sam that afternoon. Each customer waited about the same amount of time before the waitress took the order. Each of them received their meal around the same time. Each of them was served well-prepared, wholesome food. And each waited the same amount of time for the waitress to deliver the check.

But that's where the similarities ended.

Sara had walked into the coffee shop with a smile, a spring in her step and a very positive outlook on the world. It was plain for everyone to see. Her body language and her posture reflected her optimism. Sara had a delightful lunch, exchanged some pleasant conversation with the waitress, and went back to work with a re-charged battery.

Sam, on the other hand, had entered the coffee shop with a scowl on his face. He looked like he'd been sucking on sour pickles all morning. He was hunched over and tense. His body language cried out "Stay away from me!" He was annoyed when the waitress didn't take his order immediately. He was annoyed at how long it took for his meal to arrive. He complained about the food, and was furious when he didn't get his check right away.

Attitudes are a secret power working 24 hours a day, for good or bad.

— Unknown

Why did Sara and Sam have such different experiences in the coffee shop? Remember that each was treated in exactly the same way. It comes down to this: Sara sees the world with a positive attitude. Sam sees the world with a negative attitude.

A Definition Of Attitude

Think of your attitude as the mental filter through which you experience the world. Some people see the world through the filter of optimism (the glass being half full) while others see life through a filter of pessimism (the glass being half empty). Let me give you some examples to explain the difference between a positive attitude and a negative attitude.

The person with the negative attitude thinks "I CAN'T."

The person with the positive attitude thinks "I CAN."

The person with the negative attitude dwells on problems.

The person with the positive attitude concentrates on solutions.

The person with the negative attitude finds fault with others.

The person with the positive attitude looks for the good in others.

The person with the negative attitude focuses on what's missing.

The person with the positive attitude counts his or her blessings.

The person with the negative attitude sees limitations.

The person with the positive attitude sees possibilities.

I could go on and on with examples, but I'm sure you get the idea. When I talk to audiences about attitude, I often like to use word pictures. They help people to understand and remember what I said. Let me paint this picture for you: *Your attitude is your window to the world.*

Everyone Starts With A Clean Mental Window

Let's take a few moments to discuss why I say that your attitude is your window to the world. We all start out in life with a good attitude — or, should I say, a clean mental window. Just watch young children. They're always laughing and giggling. They have a sunny disposition. They love to explore new things.

Consider the attitude of a child who's learning to walk. When he stumbles and falls down, what does he do? I'll tell you what he *doesn't* do. He doesn't frown or blame the carpet. He doesn't point fingers at his mother or father for giving him lousy instructions. He doesn't quit. Oh, no. He smiles, gets up again and makes another attempt. And another. He keeps going for weeks and weeks with a positive attitude until he gets it right! His window is squeaky clean, and he feels like he can conquer the world.

> *You can't always control circumstances. But you can control your own thoughts.*
> — Charles Popplestone

But as you know, there comes a point where life starts throwing some dirt at our windows. And here's what happens:

Our windows get splattered by criticism from
   parents and teachers.

Our windows get smudged by ridicule from peers.

Our windows get smeared by rejection.

Our windows get soiled by disappointments.

Our windows get clouded by doubt.

The problem is, the dirt keeps building up, and all too many people do nothing about it. They continue to go through life with a filthy window. They lose their enthusiasm. They get frustrated and depressed. And most tragically, they give up on their dreams — all because they failed to clean their attitude window.

That's the road I was traveling down. I had a dirty window when I was an attorney. And the longer I stayed in that field, the filthier my window got. I saw no possibilities. How could I? My window was splattered with the mud of negativity.

Wash Your Window

But then, by the grace of God, I learned that all I had to do was clean off my window! I had to improve my attitude so I could see the world clearly again. After I removed the grime from my window, a whole new world opened up for me. The frustration and depression lifted. I had more confidence. For the first time in many years, I could see the magnificent possibilities that life had to offer.

And I was able to make a career transition and do work that I absolutely love. When you really think about it, I'm in the business of helping people to clean off their windows — to get a better attitude!

Do you see what I mean when I say that attitude is your window to the world? Can you appreciate how your attitude affects the way you see everything in your life? More importantly, are you beginning to see those areas where your window needs to be washed?

You Control Your Attitude

It's your job to keep your window clean. Sure, I can give you a little encouragement. And other people can encourage you, too. But in the end, nobody else can do it for you.

You see, you always have a choice. You can leave the filth on your window and look at life through a smeared glass. But there are consequences to that approach — and they're not very pretty. You'll go through life negative and frustrated. You'll be unhappy. You'll achieve only a fraction of what you're capable of achieving.

There's a better way. When you choose to take out your squeegee and clean your window, life will be brighter and sunnier. You'll be healthier and happier. You'll set some ambitious goals... and begin to achieve them. Your dreams will come alive again!

There is nothing either good or bad, but thinking makes it so.

— William Shakespeare

Still doubting whether you really have the power to change your attitude? Perhaps you're thinking, "Jeff, that's easy for you to say. Your attitude wouldn't be so good if you had my problems."

Granted, some really devastating things may have happened to you. You may have endured much suffering. Perhaps you're going through some tough times right now. But, even under the worst circumstances, I still contend that you have the power to choose your attitude. I'm not saying it's easy. But the fact remains, the choice is yours.

Let me tell you about a man who is well qualified to speak on the subject of attitude. His name is Dr. Viktor Frankl, and he went through hell on earth — and managed not only to survive... but to inspire millions of people. You see, Viktor Frankl endured years of horror as a prisoner in the Nazi death camps.

To make matters worse, his father, mother, brother and his wife died in camps or were killed in gas chambers. Every day, Frankl and the other prisoners suffered from hunger, cold and brutality. Can a person control his or her attitude in a situation like that? Here's what Dr. Frankl had to say about the importance of attitude in his best-selling book, *Man's Search For Meaning*:

"Everything can be taken from a man but one thing: the last of the human freedoms — to choose one's attitude in any given set of circumstances, to choose one's own way. ...Even though conditions such as lack of sleep, insufficient food and various mental stresses may suggest that the inmates were bound to react in certain ways, in the final analysis it becomes clear that the sort of person the prisoner became was the result of an inner decision, and not the result of camp influences alone."

A happy person is not a person in a certain set of circum- stances, but rather a person with a certain set of attitudes.

— Hugh Downs

Now, if Dr. Frankl and the other prisoners had the ability to choose their attitudes in the face of such unspeakable suffering, who are we to claim that we cannot take control of our attitudes?

As Hugh Downs has said: *"A happy person is not a person in a certain set of circumstances, but rather a person with a certain set of attitudes."* That's a powerful statement — and it's the truth.

When it's all said and done, you, and you alone, control your attitude.

Attitude And Success

Okay, let's say you clean off your window and develop a positive attitude. You're smiling. You sit home and think positive thoughts. Will that alone lead you to outrageous success and the realization of your fondest dreams? No, it won't... because there's more to success than just having a great attitude.

To maximize your potential and achieve your goals, you need to apply certain time-honored principles of success that have helped millions of people to achieve extraordinary results. And they'll do the same for you!

In the next 11 lessons of this book, I'll be taking you through these success principles, step by step. You'll learn about confronting your fears, overcoming adversity, harnessing the power of commitment and much, much more. You'll get the information and inspiration you need to start living the life you've always dreamed about.

Still, you may be wondering, what do these success principles have to do with attitude?

In a word — EVERYTHING! That's why I say *attitude is everything.*

Without a positive attitude, you can't activate the other principles. Your success in life begins and ends with your attitude.

It's only when you clean your attitude window that the other success principles can shine through. If your window is smudged, only a fraction of the light of these principles can get through. Your success is limited, or even blocked.

But when you learn to keep your attitude window clear, the light comes pouring in and you can use these empowering principles to earn more money, have more satisfying relationships, increase your spiritual awareness and reach your full potential.

When you combine a positive attitude with the other success principles, you become unstoppable!

LESSON 2 ━━━━━━━━━━━━

You're a Human Magnet

> *Whether you think you can — or think you can't — you're right!*
>
> — Henry Ford

What's the key to success? Why do some people succeed while others fail?

Earl Nightingale, the great success writer, broadcaster and speaker, addressed this issue in his famous recorded message entitled *"The Strangest Secret."* In this program, he identified the key to success in just six words. Of course, he went on to explain it in more detail — but the foundation of his success secret is only six words.

You'd like to know the six words, wouldn't you? Well, before I tell you the key to success, you might be surprised to learn that the same six words are also the key to failure!

Are you ready for the key to success? Here it is:

WE BECOME WHAT WE THINK ABOUT.

On a gut level, does that make sense to you?

In his research on the subject, Nightingale found that all

of the great writers, philosophers and religious leaders have agreed that our thoughts determine our actions. Here are the observations of a few great thinkers on this very point.

Napoleon Hill said: *"What the mind can conceive and believe, the mind can achieve."*

Nurture your mind with great thoughts.

— Benjamin Disraeli

The Bible contains numerous references to thinking, including these:

"According to your faith be it unto you." (Matthew 9:29)

"As a man thinketh in his heart, so is he." (Proverbs 23:7)

"If you can believe, all things are possible." (Mark 9:23)

Ralph Waldo Emerson put it this way: *"A man is what he thinks about all day long."*

Robert Collier offered this insight: *"There is nothing on earth you cannot have — once you have mentally accepted the fact that you can have it."*

And finally, there are the well-known words of Henry Ford, who said: *"Whether you think you can — or think you can't — you're right!"*

How This Principle Works

Let's examine this concept a little further — that WE BECOME WHAT WE THINK ABOUT. Here's how it works. If you constantly think about a particular goal, then you'll take steps to move toward that goal. Let's say that someone (whom we'll call Fred) thinks he's capable of earning $30,000 per year. Like a human magnet, Fred will attract those employment opportunities that will move him in that direction. As long as Fred clings to that thought, he'll reach his goal of earning $30,000 per year.

Now, what if Fred begins to think, "Hey, I'd like to earn more money to meet the growing needs of my family. I want to earn $50,000." Will Fred's income increase?

It depends. Just how strong is Fred's belief that he can earn $50,000? It's quite possible that Fred *would like* to earn $50,000, but he doesn't *believe* that he's really capable of earning that amount. In that case, Fred will not reach his income goal of $50,000. If, on the other hand, Fred continually thinks about earning the higher income... and believes in his ability to achieve that goal, he will, in fact, increase his income to $50,000.

As you might expect, this concept is not limited to monetary goals. Suppose you're shooting a round of 95 on the golf course right now. By concentrating on bringing that score down to 85... and by truly believing in your ability to do so... you'll begin to take steps to move toward that goal. You may take lessons. You may practice more. But in the end, you'll bring your score down and reach your objective.

Dominant Thoughts Rule The Day

The idea that *we become what we think about* has also been expressed as the Law of Dominant Thought. This means that there's a power within each of us that propels us in the direction of our current dominant thoughts.

The key word here is DOMINANT. You can't expect positive results when you spend 10 seconds a day thinking positively... and the remaining 16 waking hours dwelling on negative outcomes!

Here's the bottom line. A *little* positive thinking doesn't produce positive results. Just like a little bit of a diet doesn't work. It's like trying to lose weight by eating a healthy, low-calorie breakfast... and then pigging out on cake and ice cream for the rest of the day! The same is true of exercise — you can't do a few minutes of exercise ONCE a week and expect to be physically fit.

Look at positive thinking in the same way. *A little bit just doesn't get the job done.* Instead, you must take control of your mental activity and think positively throughout each and every day until it becomes a habit. Remember, it has to be your *dominant* thought pattern.

Take a moment to consider your dominant thoughts in

the major areas of your life. Are they serving you... or holding you back?

Attitude Adjustment Leads To Real Estate Ownership

Let me share a personal example to demonstrate the power of our thoughts. In the 1970s and early 1980s, I observed many people in my area (Long Island, New York) who were making a lot of money by purchasing homes for investment purposes — and renting them out. The homes were appreciating in value considerably each year. Sure, there were the usual headaches of having to deal with tenant problems, but the return these investors were getting was incredible!

Well, I kept thinking that I should start buying some investment homes. But I never took any action because I continued to doubt myself. My thinking was dominated by all of the things that could go wrong. Simply put, I had a lousy attitude. And with a negative attitude, is it any wonder that I never took the first step?

> *They can because they think they can.*
>
> *— Virgil*

However, after I started reading books and listening to tapes on the power of attitude and belief, I decided to change my attitude about real estate investment. In the summer of 1986, I decided that before the end of that year I would purchase two investment homes. This time, I wasn't going to allow any negative thoughts to creep into my mind.

For six months, I focused my thinking on one thing — owning two investment homes. I wrote down my goals several times each day and referred to them often. I believed, at the deepest level of my being, that I'd own two homes before the end of the year. In the evenings and on weekends, I went with real estate agents to look at homes. I personally visited about 100 homes and researched hundreds of others.

In the fall of 1986, I purchased an investment property. What a great feeling of accomplishment — to do something that I wouldn't allow myself to do before. But I still had work to do. And on December 29, just two days before the end of the year, I reached my goal and bought the second investment home.

As I look back at why I was able to purchase the real estate in 1986, while I "couldn't" do it in the years before then, the answer is clear. In 1986, I believed that I could do it. I had an unshakable positive attitude that propelled me forward to reach my goal.

This entire experience was tremendously valuable to me. In fact, it was priceless... because it taught me that you can achieve your goal when you believe in yourself and keep your thoughts focused on the positive.

Attitude Vs. Action

I've been talking a lot about *thinking* and you might be wondering where *action* fits into this process. It's true that you don't get results without action, but recognize that *thought precedes action.* I always knew the actions that I'd have to take to buy those investment properties — contact realtors, visit properties, review newspaper listings and so on. But I never took the first step as long as I had a negative attitude. The instant I changed my attitude, I felt compelled to take action... and nothing was going to stop me!

That's why a positive belief system is the starting point for the achievement of any goal. When your dominant belief is that you *can* achieve your goal, you begin taking the actions necessary to move in that direction.

Your Circumstances Reflect What You've Been Thinking About

Face this fact: Your beliefs brought you to where you are today, and your thinking from this point forward will take you to where you'll be in the future.

In fact, your results in *every* area of your life reflect your deeply held thoughts about yourself. Consider your finances. What are your beliefs in this area? Are you constantly thinking about not having enough money? Dwell on that thought (a lack of funds) and you block the flow of money to you.

And then, there's the matter of relationships. If you think that you don't deserve much, you attract friends and partners into your life who won't treat you very well. I'll bet you know someone who always seems to go out with the "wrong" person. In fact, the last 29 people they've gone out with were wrong for them. Do you think this is a mere coincidence? Oh, no. There is a deeply held belief inside that individual that attracts these people into his or her life.

And whether we're talking about finances, relationships or careers, the fact remains: *If your thoughts don't change, your results won't change.*

Change Your Thinking

Fortunately, there's exciting news. You CAN change your thoughts, thereby changing your results! Here's how. For starters, become aware of what you say to yourself all day. Each of us has an internal voice; in other words, we talk to ourselves! Too often, however, what we say is negative, critical and self-limiting. Perhaps you find yourself thinking, "I can't do this" or "I always mess things up." These thoughts work against you. Instead, repeat to yourself that you *can* and *will* accomplish your goal.

> *What we sincerely believe regarding ourselves is true for us.*
> — Orison Swett Marden

As we'll discuss more fully in Part 2 of this book, it's also important to become aware of the words you use on a regular basis. For example, do you put yourself down or talk about the things you could never have or achieve? Your mind hears every word you speak — and, like a magnet, you'll ultimately attract the events and circumstances that correspond to your dominant beliefs. So, make sure to use positive words about yourself and your goals.

Repetition Is The Key

Here are two more action steps to help you become more positive and get the results you want.

STEP 1. Every day, read some positive, uplifting literature. Find 15-30 minutes in the morning to do this — and it's also a good idea to do some reading right before bed. There are literally thousands of motivational books and articles to choose from. Read whatever speaks to you — it could be the Bible or other spiritual material, or perhaps inspiring biographies. You'll find a wide selection of success books in the Psychology and Self-Improvement section of any bookstore or library — so check them out.

STEP 2. Every day, listen to motivational audio programs. You can listen to them in your car while commuting, at home or during your exercise routine. The key is repetition. When you hear these messages over and over they become part of you — and you begin to implement them to improve your life. They will get you thinking about your attitude and other success principles on a daily basis. Of course, audio programs are not a substitute for ACTION. It's up to you to put these ideas to work!

> *Nobody succeeds beyond his or her wildest expectations unless he or she begins with some wild expectations.*
> — Ralph Charell

So, if you read something positive and listen to motivational audio programs every day, it will make a phenomenal difference in your life. I can tell you from personal experience that these techniques work if you have the discipline to stick with them.

The lesson I've learned is this: Change your thinking and you change your life! You *will* become what you think about.

Don't Count On Overnight Success
Before concluding, I'd like to clarify a few things about

positive thinking and the power of our thoughts. First of all, positive thinking doesn't mean that you'll achieve your goals overnight. It's not as if you start thinking about making more money and the next morning you wake up and find a stack of dollar bills at your bedside. *Not by a long shot.* Success requires effort, commitment and patience.

And secondly, positive thinking doesn't mean you won't have any more problems. Believe me, you'll have plenty of setbacks along the way. However, if you continue to believe in yourself, take action and persist, you'll overcome those obstacles.

Remember, you are constantly moving in the direction of your dominant thoughts. Everything you achieve in your lifetime flows from your thoughts and beliefs. Negative thinking yields negative results... and positive thinking produces positive results. Keep your attitude window clean and bright so that the positive thoughts can come shining through.

It simply makes no sense to think negative thoughts... unless you want to get negative results. And I know you don't want that to happen.

So, from this point forward, choose your thoughts wisely and use this powerful principle to get fantastic results in your life!

LESSON 3

Picture Your Way to Success!

> *You must first clearly see a thing in your mind before you can do it.*
>
> — Alex Morrison

In a television interview, singer Celine Dion was asked if she ever dreamed at the start of her career that someday she'd sell millions of records and be on tour, singing in front of tens of thousands of people each week. The singer replied that none of this surprised her, as she had pictured the whole thing since she was five years old!

She was not bragging, and has worked unbelievably hard to earn every bit of her success. What she learned at an early age was her ability to tap into the power of holding a vivid, powerful image... to picture the star she wanted to become.

World-class athletes also incorporate the power of imagery to reinforce in their mind *exactly* how they want to perform. Whether it's a figure skater completing a difficult jump... a tennis pro acing his opponent with a perfect serve... or a golfer driving the ball long and straight down the fairway, many top competitors mentally envision a successful outcome before actually achieving it in the "real" world.

Visualization, however, is not something reserved solely for singers, athletes or movie stars. In fact, it's something *you've* used since childhood to create the circumstances of your own life.

Let me clarify what I mean. Visualization is often described as "movies of the mind," "inner pictures" or "images." We all store pictures in our minds about the type of relationships we deserve, the degree of success we'll attain at work, the extent of our leadership ability, the amount of money we'll earn and accumulate, and so on.

Mental Movies From Childhood

Where do these pictures come from? Well, we begin to develop our "mental movies" early in life. If we were criticized or felt unworthy as youngsters, we record the events (and the feelings associated with those events) as images in our minds. Because we frequently dwell on these pictures (both consciously and subconsciously), we tend to create life situations that correspond to the original image.

Imagination is more important than knowledge.

— Albert Einstein

For example, you may still hold a vibrant image of being criticized by a teacher in elementary school. You felt humiliated in front of the whole class. Later on, when you were tempted to offer your opinion in school or in a group of people, you held back and kept quiet... all the while remembering (even if only on a subconscious level) how painful it was when you were criticized. The picture remains in your mind and exerts tremendous influence over your present actions.

Unfortunately, many of us have not updated or revised our childhood movies, so we're continually producing results that fall short of our full potential. What follows are some techniques for using the power of visualization to improve virtually every aspect of your life.

Take Responsibility For Your Own Movies

Not all mental pictures can be traced to your childhood. You're constantly generating mental movies based on your relationships, career experiences and other events. No matter what the source of your mental images, there's one point that I want to drive home: You — and only you — are in control of your own movies.

Let's try a short experiment. Think about an ice cream cone filled with your favorite flavor of ice cream. Does that create a picture or image for you? I'll bet it does.

Okay, now think about an elephant. Can you see it? Change the color of the elephant to pink. In a fraction of a second, you formed an image of the pink elephant. Can you bring back the picture of the ice cream cone? Of course you can.

Can you see what I mean? You have control over the pictures that occupy your mind. However, when you don't *consciously* decide which pictures to play, your mind will look into the "archives" and keep re-playing old movies on file in your mental library.

Change The Meaning Of The Old Movie

It doesn't serve you to deny what happened in a past experience, no matter how painful or disappointing. You can't, for instance, change the fact that you were criticized by the teacher. You *can*, however, alter your *interpretation* of the event.

That is, at the time you were originally criticized, the meaning you might have assigned to the experience was "I'm not good enough" or "My opinions are worthless." While this was the interpretation of a child, you may have inadvertently carried it into your adult life. Today, though, you can *consciously choose* to view the situation differently — for example, the teacher may have disagreed with you, but it wasn't a statement about your intelligence or your overall worth as a person!

Create New Pictures

We can create new mental movies whenever we choose to do so. And when we develop (and concentrate on) new images that evoke powerful feelings and sensations, we'll act in ways that support those new pictures! So, the first step is to create an image of your desired outcome. You are limited only by your imagination.

As you know, most people are terrified about public speaking. In survey after survey, it is listed as the #1 fear that people have — ranked ahead of the fear of death! So, when most people are asked to even consider making a speech, what kinds of pictures do they run through their minds? They see themselves standing nervously in front of the audience. Perhaps they're having trouble remembering what they want to say. Run these images over and over on your mental screen and you can be sure that you won't have much success as a speaker!

Instead, form a picture in your mind in which you're confidently giving your presentation. The audience members are listening to your every word. You look sharp. Your delivery is smooth. You tell a funny story and the audience is laughing. At the end, you get a warm round of applause. People come up afterward to congratulate you. Do you see how these kinds of mental images can help you to become a better speaker?

Recognize, however, that the pictures in your mind are not fulfilled overnight. But, by being patient and by persistently focusing on these mental images, you'll automatically start acting in ways that support your vision.

Picture Your Way To Sales Success

If you're involved in selling any product or service, it's vital that you see yourself succeeding on a consistent basis. If you're not getting the results you want, there's no question that you're holding onto pictures of sales mediocrity... or sales disappointment... as opposed to sales success.

Right now, think about your next meeting with a prospect. In your mind, how do you *see* the encounter? Are you confident and persuasive? Are you enthusiastically explaining the benefits of what you're offering? Is the prospect receptive and interested in what you're saying? Can you vividly see a successful outcome to your meeting?

You have control over the pictures that occupy your mind.
— Jeff Keller

Remember that you're the producer, director, script writer, lighting coordinator, costume designer and casting director of your own mental movies. You get to choose how they turn out! By mentally rehearsing and running successful outcomes through your mind, you're paving the way for success in your sales career.

Of course, if you currently run images through your mind where the prospect rejects your ideas and has no interest in your presentation, you'll attain very limited success from your sales efforts. You'll attract those people — and those situations — that correspond to your negative images.

Relax And Involve Your Senses

What's the best method to use when concentrating on your new images? It's been proven that your mind is most receptive to visualization when you're calm and not thinking about a lot of things simultaneously. So, sit down in a comfortable chair at home, close your eyes and do some deep breathing exercises to clear your mind and relax your body. Now, develop images that involve as many senses as you can. The more sights, sounds, smells, tastes and touches you put in your pictures, the more powerful the "pull" for you to make your vision a reality.

Here's an example. Let's say you've always dreamed of owning a beach-front house in the Caribbean. Picture the white and peach-colored house. See the green palm trees slowly swaying in the gentle breeze. Smell the salt air. Feel the warm sand between your toes. Feel the sunshine on your face. *Isn't this paradise?*

And all this can be yours if you hold onto this image and do what it takes to achieve it! Also, remember that those images associated with strong *emotions* have even more power, so be sure to add positive feelings to your vision. For instance, when visualizing your ideal job, combine the vivid mental picture and the physical senses with the terrific emotions of pride and satisfaction you'll have working in that new position.

Vision is the art of seeing things invisible to others.

— Jonathan Swift

Finally, don't be concerned with the quality of your images at the outset. Some people can create lively color pictures while others have trouble getting anything more than a fuzzy image. It's also possible you may only be able to get a particular *feeling* at the beginning as opposed to a clear image.

In any case, don't worry about it. Do the best you can and don't compare yourself to anyone else. Your images will become sharper over time. *The key is to spend several minutes each day running these new movies in your mind.*

Write A Check To Yourself

It's extremely powerful to formulate images of successful outcomes — and to run them through your mind. But, there's another technique you can use to accelerate your success. You can create visual aids to move you toward what you want.

In 1990, while he was still relatively unknown, comedian Jim Carrey wrote a check to himself for $10 million for "acting services rendered." The check was postdated Thanksgiving 1995. As Carrey explained, it wasn't about money. He knew that if he was making that much, he'd be working with the best people on the best material.

Carrey earned about $800,000 for his work in *Ace Ventura* and *The Mask*. Then, in late 1994, he was paid $7 million for his role in *Dumb and Dumber*. In 1995, he earned many more millions and is now getting $20 million per movie!

Jim Carrey's "postdated check" exercise is a great example of the power of the subconscious mind to actualize a goal that is held with deep conviction and feeling. Thinking about your goal and forming images in your mind will go a long way to creating the success you desire. However, when you also use a tangible representation of your goal (such as a check), your chances of success are even greater!

Now, I'm not sharing this example simply because it's an interesting story about Jim Carrey. This same technique can work for you, too!

Why not tear out one of *your* checks right now and post-date it three or five years from now with the amount that you want to earn for "services rendered"? Make sure to look at that check at least once a day... and believe that you're moving toward that goal.

Getting The Job You Want

You can use visual reminders to your advantage in a lot of ways — it's not limited to checks. Here's an example involving a friend of mine, who we'll call Robert Jones. Robert received his party's nomination for a judgeship, and he'll be on the ballot in an upcoming election.

While Robert stands an excellent chance of winning this election (and realizing his dream of becoming a judge), he's still a little nervous... and doubts creep into his mind now and again. I suggested to Robert that he make a handwritten sign that reads **JUDGE ROBERT JONES** and that he put that sign where he'll see it every day (for example, on his nightstand and on the bathroom mirror). I also recommended that he write these words on a card he can carry in his wallet.

By looking at those words throughout the day, Robert is conditioning his mind to view himself as a judge. He's going to start thinking about wearing the black robes. He'll see everyone rise as he enters the courtroom. As these images become stronger and stronger, Robert will take those actions that will bring this picture into reality. He'll campaign more. He'll make sure his party is doing everything possible to get the voters out on Election Day.

While Robert could have formed strong mental images without the use of the sign, it has so much more power with the visual aid! The sign is a reminder to Robert to think about being a judge... and to run successful images through his mind.

Of course, there are no guarantees that this will work for Robert — or that it will *always* work for you. But, once you try this for yourself, I think you'll find that it's an incredibly powerful aid to help you get what you want!

If you can dream it, you can do it.

— Walt Disney

So, is there a position that you want to achieve? Sales manager... supervisor... attorney... owner of your own business? Whatever it is, create a visual aid and your mind will get to work to bring that picture into your life.

It Works Both Ways

Be very careful when using visual reminders. Some people use negative aids — and with very serious consequences. Bumper stickers offer a prime example.

While riding in my car a few years ago, I noticed a bumper sticker on the car in front of me. The bumper sticker read, *"I owe, I owe, so off to work I go."* In the last few years, I've seen this same bumper sticker over and over. It's obviously quite popular. Just a silly little rhyme, right? A harmless joke?

Wrong! There's nothing funny or harmless about this message. When you put something like that on your car, you are programming your mind to keep you in debt!

Think about someone who puts this bumper sticker on her car. We'll call her Alice. Every morning, Alice steps outside to greet the day and sees the statement "I owe." When it's time to leave work, she goes back to her car and sees "I owe." This idea will become embedded in her subconscious mind. She'll form mental pictures associated with being in debt. And, if you recall Lesson 2, Alice will always attract what she thinks about most. In this case, she will attract lots and lots of debt.

If you ask Alice why she never has enough money, she'll say that she has bad luck. The truth is, Alice is careless about what goes into her mind. The "harmless" little bumper sticker of today becomes your reality tomorrow.

Alice is a perfect example of someone throwing more mud on an already dirty attitude window. If *attitude is everything*, then Alice's predominant attitude is "I'm a debtor!" With an attitude like that, what do you think her future will bring — prosperity... or more debt?

We both know the answer to that question.

Lights... Camera... Action

Well, there you have it — some suggestions for creating and benefiting from your own mental movies. Remember, if you don't take control and develop your own movies, you'll continue to replay the old ones. If the old movies are serving you, that's great. But if they're holding you back in any way, get started *today* and use the incredible power of your mind to picture your way to greater success!

LESSON 4 ————————————————

Make a Commitment... and You'll Move Mountains!

> *What this power is I cannot say; all I know is that it exists and it becomes available only when a man is in that state of mind in which he knows exactly what he wants and is fully determined not to quit until he finds it.*
>
> — Alexander Graham Bell

I used to think I knew what commitment and persistence meant. *Trying hard. Making a lot of attempts.* However, I didn't grasp the true meaning of these concepts until I read a small paperback book entitled *The Ultimate Secret To Getting Absolutely Everything You Want,* by Mike Hernacki.

Commitment is the essence of *The Ultimate Secret.* According to the author, the key to getting what you want is the *"willingness to do whatever it takes"* to accomplish your objective. Now, before your mind jumps to conclusions, let me add that in saying *"whatever it takes"* I exclude all actions which are illegal, unethical or which harm other people.

So, exactly what do I mean by this "willingness"? It's a mental attitude that says:

If it takes 5 steps to reach my goal, I'll take those 5 steps;
If it takes 55 steps to reach my goal, I'll take those 55 steps;
If it takes 155 steps to reach my goal, I'll take those 155 steps.

Of course, at the outset, you usually won't know exactly how many steps will be required to reach your goal. This doesn't matter. To succeed, all that's necessary is that you make a commitment to do whatever it takes — regardless of the number of steps involved.

Where does persistence fit in? Persistent action follows commitment — that is, you first must be committed to something before you'll persist to achieve it. Once you've made a commitment to achieve your goal, then you'll follow through with relentless determination and action until you attain the desired result.

The "Magic" Of Commitment

When you make a commitment and are willing to do whatever it takes, you begin to attract the people and circumstances necessary to accomplish your goal. For instance, once you devote yourself to becoming, say, a best-selling author, you might suddenly "bump into" a literary agent or "discover" a television program offering advice on this very topic.

It's not as if these resources never existed before. It's just that your mind never focused on finding them. Once you commit yourself to something, you create a mental picture of what it would be like to achieve it. Then, your mind immediately goes to work, like a magnet, attracting events and circumstances that will help bring your picture into reality. It's important to realize, however, that this is not an overnight process; you must be *active* and seize the opportunities as they appear.

The magic which flows from commitment has never been more eloquently or more accurately described than in the following words by W. H. Murray:

"Until one is committed there is hesitancy, the chance to draw back, always ineffectiveness. Concerning all acts of initiative (and creation) there is one elementary truth, the ignorance of which kills countless ideas and splendid plans; that the moment one definitely commits oneself, then Providence moves, too.

"All sorts of things occur to help one that would otherwise never have occurred. A whole stream of events issues from the

decision, raising in one's favor all manner of unforeseen incidents and meetings and material assistance, which no man could have dreamt would have come his way."

Doors Will Open

Here's another miraculous feature of the power of commitment: You don't have to know at the outset *how* to achieve your goal. Sure, you'll be better off if you have a plan of attack, but it's not essential that every step be mapped out in advance.

Effort only fully releases its reward after a person refuses to quit.

— *Napoleon Hill*

In fact, when you have the willingness to do whatever it takes, the "right" steps are often suddenly revealed to you. You'll meet people you never could have planned to meet. Doors will unexpectedly open for you. It might seem like luck or good fortune is smiling on you; in truth, you'll have created these positive events by making a commitment and, thus, instructing your mind to look for them.

Here's an example of how a door unexpectedly opened for me. In 1989, I started writing motivational articles. I'd learned about the power of a positive attitude and the other success principles, and I was committed to sharing this information with others who could benefit from it. But I had no idea where to start. Do I send my articles to newspapers... submit them to magazines... write my own book?

The first thing I did was submit an article to a local newsletter for people involved in training and human resources. That article was printed in the summer of 1990. A few months later, I got a phone call from a gentleman named Stuart Kamen, a freelance writer who also worked with businesses to produce newsletters. Stuart said he'd seen my article while visiting the home of his best friend — and was very impressed with it.

Then he asked me, "Have you ever thought of writing a newsletter?" Quite frankly, I hadn't thought of doing my own newsletter. We arranged a meeting and Stuart explained how we could work together to produce a newsletter that would make these self-development concepts available to thousands of people.

About one month later, the first issue of *Attitude is Everything* newsletter was published. And we've been going strong for nearly 20 years — and have reached hundreds of thousands of people with this life-changing information!

> *With ordinary talent and extraordinary perseverance, all things are attainable.*
>
> — Sir Thomas Buxton

How did it all happen? I was *committed* to sharing these principles with others. I had a positive attitude. I started writing. And then, Stuart Kamen, a complete stranger, entered my life — someone who knew just how to turn my dream into reality.

Ah, the magic of commitment!

A Word Of Caution

Before you get too excited about waltzing easily toward your goals, I caution you. Even with a commitment, everything won't be rosy on your path. Life will test you to see how serious you are about achieving your objective. Obstacles will arise. You'll make mistakes and suffer disappointments and setbacks, some of which may be quite severe and even tempt you to abandon your goal.

That's when it becomes important to follow the sage wisdom of Winston Churchill, who said: *"Never, never, never give up."* Or the advice provided by James J. Corbett: *"You become a champion by fighting one more round. When things are tough, you fight one more round."*

If you've made a commitment to accomplish a goal, you *can* overcome temporary defeats... and you *will* triumph!

Commitment Pays Off For Aspiring Novelist

Several years ago, *American Way* magazine carried a fascinating interview with best-selling novelist David Baldacci. Baldacci is the author of the immensely successful novels *Absolute Power*, *Total Control* and *The Winner*. Millions of copies of his books have been sold.

Let me assure you, however, that Baldacci was no overnight success. His accomplishments and financial achievements were the result of his total commitment to developing his talents as a writer. Like me, Baldacci started out as a lawyer. He started law school in 1983 and didn't give any thought to becoming a best-selling novelist. He simply enjoyed writing.

Yet, at the outset, Baldacci knew that he didn't have the necessary writing skills. So he made a commitment, as he put it, to learn the craft of writing. For the first five years, he didn't finish any of his projects. Every day, he just worked on characters, plot development and other writing basics.

At the time, he was a practicing lawyer, and he and his wife had two young children. When did he find the time to do this writing? Baldacci worked on his writing every night from 10:00 pm until 2:00 am. Now, that's a commitment to do whatever it takes! He pointed out, however, that he had fun writing — it wasn't a chore. By the way, I'm not suggesting that you stay up all night to pursue your goals — that 10:00 pm to 2:00 am shift certainly wouldn't work for me, and it may not work for you, either!

After 10 years of writing, Baldacci had completed some short stories and a few screenplays. His total sales: ZERO. All that he had to show for his efforts were a lot of rejections from editors.

In 1996, all of Baldacci's efforts paid off... big time! He received millions of dollars for the literary and movie rights to his blockbuster thriller *Absolute Power*. The star of the movie was Clint Eastwood.

> *One person with a commitment is worth more than 100 people who have only an interest.*
>
> — Mary Crowley

Such is the power of a person who is committed.

He Refused To Quit

I've learned a lot about the magic of commitment from my good friend, Jerry Gladstone. In 1986, Jerry started his own company, American Royal Arts, selling a variety of collectibles. One year later, he decided to concentrate on selling animation art. He secured licenses with Warner Brothers, Hanna Barbera and other, smaller studios. But he realized that to really grow his business, he needed to sell Disney art.

For three years, he wrote letters and called Disney headquarters requesting permission to sell Disney art. Each time, he got the same answer from Disney: NO.

That didn't stop Jerry. He kept contacting Disney executives. One executive finally had just about all she could take of Jerry. So she told him, in a voice and tone reminiscent of Maleficent from *Sleeping Beauty*, the evil queen from *Snow White* and Cruella DeVil from *101 Dalmatians* all rolled into one, "You'll never get a Disney license!"

Time to give up, right? Not Jerry! Through all these rejections, he kept a great attitude. He called more executives at Disney. And then one gentleman at Disney, hoping to get rid of Jerry once and for all, said, "Well, the only two places we would consider allowing a gallery offering Disney artwork to open would be either Minnesota or Massachusetts."

Jerry's business was in New York, and he had no desire to open a gallery in a remote location. Guess what Jerry did? He flew to Boston the very next day. And by the end of the day, he had signed a lease for a place on Newbury Street in Boston!

> *The rewards for those who persevere far exceed the pain that must precede the victory.*
> — Ted Engstrom

He called the Disney executive to report that he had the Massachusetts location. They both had a good laugh. And then the executive said to Jerry, "If you had the courage to go up to Boston the next day and open a place just like that, we have to put you on the Disney program." Within a few weeks, Jerry opened the Boston gallery featuring the Disney line.

Within a year, he was given permission to market the

Disney line through his New York store. Jerry has now done business with Disney for decades. He has sold millions of dollars of Disney art and is the largest volume Disney animation art dealer in the world!

Talk about commitment... talk about keeping a good attitude in the face of rejection! Jerry was going to get the Disney license no matter what it took. Just ask Jerry, and he'll tell you "in a New York minute" that *attitude is everything!*

As Long As It Takes

I'd like to share with you the story of Benjamin Roll, who lives in Newport Beach, California. In 1990, at the age of 67, Roll graduated from law school. Naturally, before he could start practicing law, he had to pass the California Bar Examination.

On his first attempt at the examination, he failed. On his second attempt, he failed. And he failed the third time... the fourth time... the fifth time... the sixth time... the seventh time... the eighth time... the ninth time... the 10th time... the 11th time... the 12th time... and the 13th time.

Let me add one important fact: the Bar Examination is given only twice each year. So, at the time of his 13th failed attempt, Roll was now 73 years old. Most people would have quit, but not Benjamin Roll!

He took the exam for the 14th time... and he passed! In 1997, at the age of 74, Roll was admitted to practice law in the state of California. Now, here's a guy who's committed... and willing to do whatever it takes. As Roll explained, "I was going to pass that cotton-pickin' exam if I lived long enough. And I did!"

Does this story tell you anything about the importance of attitude? Most people wouldn't even consider starting law school in their 60s. Yet, here's someone who not only enrolled in law school, but was willing to spend six years after graduation studying to pass the Bar Exam.

Wow! Benjamin Roll's story is simply further proof that *attitude is everything!*

Time To Make A Commitment

Now, let's assume you have a goal in mind. The next question to ask yourself is, "Am I willing to do whatever it takes to achieve this goal?" If your answer is, "I'll do just about anything, except that I won't do _____ ," then frankly, you're not committed.

And if you're not committed, it's likely that you'll be derailed and not achieve your objective. For instance, many people start a new business with this approach: "I'll give it six months to prosper. If things don't work out after six months, I'll quit." This is not a mental attitude that leads to success.

Where would novelist David Baldacci be if he had said, "I'll try the writing for one year... and if I can't sell anything, I'll give it up"? He'd have missed out on the opportunity to do what he loves... have financial independence... and live his dream!

Now, I'm not suggesting that you just bull ahead without a plan and hope for the best. Of course you should set timetables, deadlines and budgets so you stay on course and succeed as quickly as possible. But the reality is, despite your most careful plans, you don't know how long it will take to achieve your goal... and you can't foresee all the obstacles that will cross your path.

That's where commitment separates the winners from the losers. The committed people are going to hang in — and prevail — no matter what. And if it takes a little longer than they thought, so be it. Those who aren't committed are going to give up the ship when things don't go their way.

Now that you've learned about the power of commitment, it's time to apply the principle. So, go ahead. Select a goal you have a burning desire to achieve. Make a commitment to do *whatever it takes* to achieve this goal. Start moving forward and get ready to notice and take advantage of all opportunities that come your way. Then follow through with persistent action and get ready to succeed!

LESSON 5 ———————————

Turn Your Problems into Opportunities

Every adversity carries with it the seed of an equivalent or greater benefit.

— Napoleon Hill

When faced with problems or setbacks in your life, what is your immediate reaction? If you're like most people, your first impulse is to complain. "Why did this have to happen to me? What am I going to do now? My plans are ruined!"

This response is only natural. However, after the initial disappointment wears off, you have a choice to make. You can either wallow in misery and dwell on the negative aspects of your situation *or* you can find the benefit or lesson that the problem is offering.

Yes, you'll probably face a period of uncertainty or struggle, but there's always a flip side to the difficulty. You see, a "problem" is often not a problem at all. *It may actually be an opportunity*. For instance, a problem may point out an adjustment you can make to improve certain conditions in your life. Without the problem, you never would have taken this positive action.

For example, you probably know or have heard about someone who lost his or her job and then went on to start a successful business. Often, that person will tell you that if he or she hadn't been laid off, the new business would never have been started. What started as an adversity ended up as a golden opportunity.

How about the times you were absolutely convinced that a particular job was perfect for you; you had a great interview and just couldn't wait for the offer. But the offer never came — someone else got the job. You were devastated! Days or months later a new job came along, and you realized that the first position was much less desirable than the one that came along later. The earlier rejection was, in fact, a blessing. Another example is the deal on the "dream house" which falls through... only to be replaced by something even better.

Finding the Benefit

The *New York Times* printed an essay, "Is There Meaning to a Brain Tumor?" written by a 40-year-old woman named Sharon who was told that she had a large tumor behind her left eye. The tumor was surgically removed in a six-hour operation. Fortunately, it was benign. Can you imagine someone finding a host of benefits in this frightening situation? According to Sharon, there have been many positives.

Sharon was deeply touched by the outpouring of help and support the community gave to her and her family during this crisis. People in the community, some of whom were only acquaintances, provided evening meals for her husband and their children. Her friends made arrangements for her house to be cleaned. Sharon learned about the human capacity for kindness and for helping others in time of need.

Having confronted the fragility of her own life, Sharon now says that she developed a more positive attitude and is eager to accomplish the goals she set while lying in her hospital bed. She also has developed a closer, more meaningful relationship with her brother and sister. As Sharon explained, it took a personal misfortune for her to see how good life can be. She has gained a new appreciation and zest for living by overcoming a trying and difficult experience.

From Tragedy To Triumph

The road to success often travels through adversity. Just ask entrepreneur Dave Bruno. In the 1980s, Bruno worked his way up to national sales manager for a medical equipment company. He and his wife, Marlene, and their three young children lived in a lovely suburban home in Milwaukee. Things were looking good.

But in 1984 Bruno lost his job. And several months later — while still out of work — Dave Bruno was driving home at night when his car veered off the road and crashed. He suffered massive injuries, including collapsed lungs, broken ribs, a bruised heart, a ruptured spleen and a lacerated liver.

The doctors didn't know if he would live. Bruno himself thought he was going to die. After tenuously clinging to a life support system for three days, he was miraculously in the clear. Bruno felt like he'd been given a second chance.

While recovering in the hospital, he started to think about what he would do with his life. Prior to the accident, and indeed for most of his life, he had collected motivational and inspirational quotes. He had learned as a youngster the amazing power quotations could hold, as his mother had a habit of strategically placing them throughout the house and on the refrigerator. They always lifted his spirits and provided direction.

No pressure, no diamonds.

— Mary Case

Suddenly, he had a flash of insight about what to do. He'd start a business to share these quotations with others, so they, too, could be inspired. But he didn't have a clue about how to do it.

And after he got out of the hospital there was more bleak news. Because of astronomical medical bills and the inability to work, Bruno had to declare bankruptcy. He and his family lost their home and moved into a cramped apartment.

Yet Bruno would not give up on his dream. He pushed onward, with a positive attitude and relentless determination. Over the next few years, he took jobs where he could learn about marketing and printing. He was always looking for a vehicle for his quotations.

One day, an idea hit him like a ton of bricks: He'd print the quotations on credit card stock. Later that evening, he was watching TV and saw a commercial for a credit card company's "gold card."

Even better, he thought. Print the quotes on metallic gold cards that people could take with them wherever they went. So, he created a series of quotations on topics such as attitude, leadership, persistence and courage. He called them Success Gold Cards.

> *The things which hurt,*
> *instruct.*
> — Benjamin Franklin

Five years after leaving the hospital, Dave Bruno sold his first Success Gold Card. And, I'm happy to report that he's now sold more than two million of those cards!

Dave Bruno turned a tragic accident into an incredible triumph.

Business Disappointment Is Blessing In Disguise

Now, I don't want you to think that this principle only applies to tragedies, because nothing could be further from the truth. I'd like to share a business example that reinforced my faith in this concept. In March of 1991, after an exhaustive search, I selected a company to screen print my *Attitude is Everything* T-shirts.

In late June, I committed myself to a local and national advertising campaign to market these shirts. A serious issue developed in early July. Instead of filling an order in two weeks (as originally promised), the screen printer didn't fill the order for more than five weeks. This was unacceptable, and I decided to find another screen printer.

But I'd already established my pricing and delivery terms based on discussions with the original printer. This was a *major problem*, right? What if I couldn't find another company to deliver a product of equal quality at or near the same price?

Well, rather than get depressed and curse my rotten luck, I immediately set out to get another, *better* printer. Within one week, I found the printer I was looking for. Now, instead of having an order filled in two to five weeks, it

> *It is a rough road that leads to the heights of greatness.*
> — *Seneca*

is filled in two to four *days*. Nearly 20 years later, I'm still working with this vendor.

Losing the first screen printer was the best thing that could have happened! Of course, I didn't know it at the time, but I kept believing that I could make this seemingly "bad situation" turn out to my advantage. And I did. Experiences like this have taught me that when one door shuts, there is always a better one waiting to be opened.

Career Change Emerges From Frustration

My own career transition is another example of how benefits come from problems and difficulties. I was never interested in self-development materials until I had years of unhappiness after graduating from law school. I only found these principles after I'd reached a low point in my life.

I now realize that all the miseries I endured were really blessings in disguise! I can see, quite clearly, how the events of my life "set me up" for what was to come. I had to go through the tough times and the unhappiness — and to break through that low mood so I would understand the power of a positive attitude.

So, when someone tells me they're discouraged, or it's obvious they have a negative attitude, I know what that feels like. I've been there! By going through some challenging times, I learned things that are invaluable to me — and I can relate much better to those who hear my presentations and read my writings.

And the reality is, if I hadn't grown more and more dissatisfied with my work as an attorney, I never would have been open to switching careers. If I had rated my job as a "C" or "C-," I would have kept practicing law. I would have settled for living a "C" life. It's only because I was a "D-"... and heading for an "F"... that I was motivated to make a change!

Adversity brings out our hidden potential.

— Jeff Keller

When someone asks me why I changed careers, I reply, without hesitation, "LOTS OF PAIN" — physically, emotionally and spiritually. And it's that pain — too intense to ignore — that forced me to make a decision and move in another direction. Life is now an "A"... and things are only getting better!

Now, let's look at your life. Can you think of any situations where a seemingly negative experience turned into something positive?

Maybe you were dismissed from a job... and then landed a better position. Or, perhaps you had a health problem and it caused you to change your diet or to start exercising regularly. Carefully review the difficulties and setbacks you've faced — and identify the benefits and lessons that came out of these experiences. The positives are there... if you look for them!

How Adversity Serves Us

At this point, let's examine seven ways in which adversity can serve us.

1. *Adversity gives us perspective.* Once you've recovered from a life-threatening illness, a flat tire or a leaky roof doesn't seem so troubling anymore. You're able to rise above the petty annoyances of daily living and focus your attention on the truly important things in your life.

2. *Adversity teaches us to be grateful.* Through problems and difficulties, especially those which involve loss or

deprivation, you develop a deeper appreciation for many aspects of your life. It's trite but true — you don't usually appreciate something until it's taken away from you. When you have no hot water, you suddenly value hot water. Not until you're sick do you cherish good health. The wise person continues to dwell on blessings, even after the period of loss or deprivation has passed. Remember, we're always moving in the direction of our dominant thoughts; therefore, concentrating on what you have to be grateful for brings even more good things into your life.

3. *Adversity brings out our hidden potential.* After surviving a difficult ordeal or overcoming an obstacle, you emerge emotionally stronger. Life has tested you and you were equal to the task. Then, when the next hurdle appears, you're better equipped to handle it. Problems and challenges bring out the best within us — we discover abilities we never knew we possessed. Many of us would never have discovered these talents if life hadn't made us travel over some bumpy ground. Adversity reveals to you your own strengths and capacities, and beckons you to develop those qualities even further.

4. *Adversity encourages us to make changes and take action.* Most people cling to old, familiar patterns regardless of how boring or painful their lives have become. It often takes a crisis or a series of difficulties to motivate them to make adjustments. Problems are often life's way of letting you know that you're off course and need to take corrective action.

5. *Adversity teaches us valuable lessons.* Take the example of a failed business venture: The entrepreneur may learn something that enables him or her to succeed spectacularly on the next venture.

6. *Adversity opens a new door.* A relationship terminates and you go on to a more satisfying relationship. You lose your job and find a better one. In these instances, the "problem" is not a problem at all, but rather an opportunity in disguise. One door in your life has been shut, but there is a better one waiting to be opened.

7. *Adversity builds confidence and self-esteem.* When you muster all of your courage and determination to overcome an obstacle, you feel competent and gain confidence. You have a greater feeling of self-worth and you carry these positive feelings into subsequent activities.

Look For The Positive

Sure, you'll have your share of problems and adversities in life. I'm not suggesting that when tragedy strikes you deny your emotions or refuse to face reality. What I *am* saying is don't immediately judge your situation as a tragedy and dwell on how bad off you are. Sometimes you won't be able to instantly spot the benefit that will come from being in your situation... but it *does* exist.

You always have a choice. You can view your problems as negative and become gloomy and depressed about them. Let me assure you this approach will only make things worse. Or, you can see every seemingly negative experience in your life as an opportunity... as something you can learn from... as something you can grow from. Believe it or not, your problems are there to serve you — not to destroy you!

So, the next time you suffer a problem or setback in your life, don't get discouraged or give up. Don't let problems cloud your attitude window forever. Clear off that cloudy window. You may find, after the dust settles, that you can actually see better than you did before! Just remember the words of Napoleon Hill: *"Every adversity carries with it the seed of an equivalent or greater benefit."*

Continually ask yourself what you've learned from your trying experience and focus on moving forward and growing as a person. In times of crisis, always strive to maintain an optimistic attitude and an open mind — for this is the environment that will allow you to find the benefit in your difficulty.

PART 2 ━━━━━━━━━━━━━━━━

Watch Your Words

Repeat anything often enough and it will start to become you.

— Tom Hopkins

LESSON 6 ⎯⎯⎯⎯⎯⎯

Your Words Blaze
a Trail

> *The words you consistently select will shape your destiny.*
>
> — Anthony Robbins

When was the last time you seriously thought about the words you use each and every day? How carefully do you select them?

Now, you might be thinking, "Jeff, why all this fuss about words? What's the big deal?" The answer is simple. Your words have incredible power. They can build a bright future, destroy opportunity or help maintain the status quo. Your words reinforce your beliefs… and your beliefs create your reality.

Think of this process as a row of dominos that looks like this:

THOUGHTS **❯** WORDS **❯** BELIEFS **❯** ACTIONS **❯** RESULTS

Here's how it works. Tom has a THOUGHT, such as "I'm not very good when it comes to sales." Now, let's remember that he doesn't have this thought only once. Oh, no. He's run it through his mind on a regular basis, maybe hundreds or thousands of times in his life!

Then, Tom starts to use WORDS that support this thought. He says to his friends and colleagues, "I'm never going to do very well in sales" or "I just hate making sales calls or approaching prospects." Here again, Tom repeats these phrases over and over... in his self-talk and in his discussions with others.

This, in turn, strengthens his BELIEFS — and it's at this stage where the rubber really meets the road. You see, everything that you'll achieve in your life flows from your beliefs. So, in our sales example, Tom develops the belief that he's not going to be successful in sales and that he won't earn much money. This becomes embedded in his subconscious mind.

What can possibly flow from that belief? Because Tom doesn't believe in his sales ability, he takes very little ACTION, or he takes actions that aren't productive. He doesn't do the things that would be necessary to succeed in sales.

And then, quite predictably, Tom gets very poor RESULTS.

To make matters worse, Tom then starts to think more negative thoughts... repeat more negative words... reinforce negative beliefs... and get even more negative results. It's a vicious cycle!

Words are, of course, the most powerful drug used by mankind.

— Rudyard Kipling

Of course, this whole process could have had a very happy ending if Tom had selected positive THOUGHTS... and reinforced them with positive WORDS. In turn, he'd reinforce the BELIEF that he's successful in sales. As a result, Tom would take the ACTIONS consistent with that belief... and wind up with outstanding RESULTS.

My point is don't underestimate the role of your WORDS in this process. People who feed themselves a steady diet of negative words are destined to have a negative attitude.

It's a simple matter of cause and effect. You can't keep repeating negative words and expect to be a high achiever. And that's because negative words will always lead to the reinforcement of negative beliefs — and eventually to negative outcomes.

Why You Don't Want Me To Fix Anything In Your Home

When it comes to home repairs, I'm lost. You want me to replace a faucet or fix something in the toilet tank? I'd have a better chance of reaching the top of Mount Everest. Carpentry or electrical wiring? I haven't got a clue. You want to know my ultimate Achilles heel? It's those instruction sheets that explain how to assemble something that you've just taken out of the box. You know what I mean — those black and white booklets with references to "Figure 10A" that show you (or claim to show you!) where all the nuts and bolts go... and how all the parts fit together.

Instruction sheets have the same affect on me as kryptonite had on Superman. If you recall the old Superman programs, the villain would shoot bullets at Superman — and the bullets bounced off his chest harmlessly. But there was one substance that Superman could not defend against — kryptonite. Whenever the bad guy held up a piece of kryptonite, Superman got wobbly and began to lose his power.

Well, when I see an instruction sheet, I get weak in the knees and lose my power. I just know it's useless for me to even look at it. There's no way I'm going to understand it. So I put down the instructions and yell for Dolores to come in and show me what to do. For Dolores, it's a piece of cake.

How did it come to this? I don't claim to be the smartest guy in the world, but I consider myself to be reasonably intelligent. Am I missing some gene for home repair skills that other people were given? No, that's not it, either.

The answer is quite obvious. For the last 40 years, I have repeatedly said, "I'm no good at mechanical things" and "I can't fix anything." And, lo and behold, after 40 years of using negative words, I've developed a strong belief that I can't do these things.

Do you see how I created this situation by not being careful about the words I used? And, the truth is I could eventually reverse this trend if I'd start using positive words about my ability to make repairs.

Scientist's Words Are Worth Looking At

Years ago, I read an article about Kent Cullers, a scientist who headed NASA's Search for Extra Terrestrial Intelligence project. Cullers, who has a doctorate in physics, was developing software that searches for radio signals indicating the presence of other life forms in the universe.

Sounds a little like *Star Trek*, doesn't it? But make no mistake about it, this is some pretty technical scientific research.

And yet, Cullers has a physical challenge to contend with. Let me tell you how he describes it. He refers to his condition as "a trivial affliction" and "just barely an inconvenience." What is Cullers' particular physical challenge? A touch of arthritis? Or an occasional migraine headache?

Kent Cullers is blind. That's right... he's blind. Isn't it incredible that someone can describe blindness as "a trivial affliction" or "just barely an inconvenience"?

In words are seen the state of mind, character and disposition of the speaker.

— Plutarch

By using these words, Kent Cullers is empowering himself to achieve great things. He doesn't give any power to his limitations and, as a result, he is able to transcend them and accomplish more than those who have their sight.

What obstacles are you facing in your life right now? Imagine the power you could unleash if you saw them as "just barely an inconvenience" instead of as an insurmountable barrier.

To Tell... Or Not To Tell

When I speak about the importance of using positive language to move you toward your goals, some of you may be wondering, "Jeff, do I say these positive words to myself or do I also say these words to other people?" You may be afraid that if you tell others about your goals, they'll think you're being conceited — and they may even laugh at you.

Allow me to suggest a few guidelines in this area, with the understanding that there are no "hard and fast" rules — and you should do what works best for you.

To begin with, use positive self-talk as often as possible. In my view, the more the merrier. After all, you're talking to yourself, so you don't have to worry about others hearing your comments. The key is that *you* hear this positive input again and again... and it becomes deeply rooted in your subconscious mind.

Whether to share your goals with other people is a much trickier issue. One thing I've learned is this: *Never discuss your goals with negative people.* All they'll do is argue and point out all the reasons why you won't be successful. Who needs that? Often, these "negative nellies" are the ones who do little or nothing in their own lives. They have no goals or dreams — and they don't want anyone else to succeed, either.

Yet, there are some instances when you *can* benefit by telling others about your goals. First of all, make sure that you're speaking with someone who's extremely positive and totally supportive of your efforts. This should be the kind of person who would be absolutely delighted if you achieved this goal... and would do anything in his or her power to assist you. You may have a friend or colleague that fits this role — or certain family members.

It's also important to share your goals with others who are working with you to achieve that outcome. For example, if a sales manager wants to increase sales in the coming year by 20 percent, he or she would make this goal known to everyone on the staff. Then, everyone can work together to achieve it.

Even though I'm encouraging you to use positive words to move you toward your objectives, I'm not suggesting that you ignore the obstacles that you may face — or that you discourage feedback from other people. Before embarking on any goal, you want to prepare for what may be coming down the road. Personally, I prefer to discuss those issues with someone who is positive... someone whose feedback includes creative solutions to the difficulties that may arise.

Furthermore, I'll only discuss my plans with people who are qualified to render an intelligent opinion on the subject. If you're thinking of going into your own business, it simply makes no sense to consult with your Uncle Elmer, especially if Uncle Elmer is negative and worked for someone else all of his life. What does he know about owning a business? He'll give you a list of reasons NOT to go into business for yourself. After your little chat with Uncle Elmer, you'll start to doubt yourself. You don't need that kind of help!

Words And Accountability

There's another reason why, in some cases, you might decide to share your goal with someone else. And that's for accountability. In other words, if I tell others I'm going to do something, then I have to go ahead and do it! Think of this approach as "burning your bridges."

Let me assure you I'm not a believer in "burning bridges" when it comes to personal or business relationships. But sometimes the only way to move forward in life — and to achieve an ambitious goal — is to cut off all avenues of retreat.

This can be a very useful strategy. We may tell a friend that we're going to work out at the gym three times this week — knowing that at the end of the week, this friend will ask whether we did, in fact, go to the gym three times!

An even more dramatic example is that of well-known motivational speaker Zig Ziglar. Ziglar decided to go on a diet and reduce his weight from 202 pounds to 165 pounds. At the same time, he was writing his book *See You At The Top*.

In the book, Ziglar included a statement that he got his weight down to 165 pounds. This was 10 months *before* the book went to press. And then he placed an order with the printer for 25,000 copies! Now, remember, at the time he wrote these words, Ziglar actually weighed 202. He put his credibility on the line with 25,000 people!

By including a statement that he weighed 165 pounds, Ziglar knew that he had to lose 37 pounds before the book was printed. And, he did!

Use this strategy selectively. Limit it to those goals that are very important to you — and where you're committed to go the distance. Is it risky? You bet it is. But it's a tremendous motivator!

> *The people who always talk about a lack of money generally don't accumulate much of it.*
> — *Jeff Keller*

Words And Emotions

In his best-selling book *Awaken the Giant Within*, Anthony Robbins devotes an entire chapter to the way in which our vocabulary affects our emotions, our beliefs and our effectiveness in life. I don't agree with all of Robbins' philosophies, but his observations about the power of words are right on the mark. Robbins is keenly aware of how certain words impact our emotional intensity.

For instance, let's say that someone has lied to you. You could react by saying that you're "angry" or "upset." If, however, you used the words "furious," "livid" or "enraged," your physiology and your subsequent behavior would be dramatically altered. Your blood pressure would rise. Your face would turn beet red. You'd feel tense all over.

On the other hand, what if you characterized the situation as "annoying" or said that you were "peeved"? This lowers your emotional intensity considerably. In fact, saying that you are "peeved," explains Robbins, will probably make you laugh — and break the negative emotional cycle completely. You'd be much more relaxed.

Robbins gives other examples of how you can lower the intensity of negative emotions. Imagine, for instance, replacing "I've been destroyed" with "I've been set back"... or using the phrase "I prefer" instead of "I hate." Of course, you can also intentionally select words to heighten *positive* emotions. Instead of saying "I'm determined," why not say "I'm unstoppable!" Or, in place of declaring that you "feel okay," try "I feel phenomenal!" or "I feel just tremendous!"

Choose words that will point you in the direction of your goals.
— *Jeff Keller*

Juicy, exciting words like that lift your spirits to a higher level and profoundly influence those around you. When you consciously decide to use such terms, you're actually choosing to change the path on which you've been traveling. Others will respond to you differently and you'll alter your perception of yourself, as well.

A Closer Look At Your Words

Let's take a look at your life for a moment. Are there any areas where you've been using phrases like "I can't," "I'm no good at ____" and "It's impossible"? We all know people who make statements like these:

I can't draw.
I'm no good at math.
I can't remember names.
It's impossible for me to make that kind of money.

When you make these comments day in and day out for 10, 20 or 30 years, you're programming your mind for failure! *It all comes back to your attitude.* Every one of these examples reflects a negative attitude. And if you see the world through a smudged window, you're going to use negative language... and get disappointing results.

Fortunately, you can control your words — which means that you have the ability to build a positive belief system... and to produce the results *you want.* The first step is awareness. Let's examine the phrases you've been using in four key areas of your life — relationships, finances, career and health.

1. Relationships

Do you say things like "All the good men (or women) are taken!" or "People are always taking advantage of me!" If you do, you're literally programming yourself for unhappy relationships. Your mind hears every word you speak and it sets out to prove you right. With regard to our above examples, your mind will see to it that you attract only those persons who will disappoint you or take advantage of you. Is this what you want? If not, stop repeating (and causing your mind to focus on) such negative statements!

2. Finances

What words do you use on a regular basis to describe your current financial situation and your prospects for the future? Phrases such as "I'm always in debt," "The economy is lousy" or "No one is buying" work against you. Far better to choose language which reaffirms prosperity and better economic times. Of course, you won't necessarily have abundant wealth within a few days after changing the way you speak. But the physical conditions can change only *after* your beliefs have altered. Clearing up your language is an important first step!

After all, the people with wealth in this world didn't get that way by moaning about being in poverty. And the people who always talk about a lack of money generally don't accumulate much of it.

3. Career

If I were to ask you about your career prospects over the next five to 10 years, how would you respond? Be honest. Would you say that things will probably remain the same as they are now? Or would you describe a higher position with more challenges, more responsibilities and increased financial rewards? If you respond "I don't know where I'm going in my career," chances are not much will change. Your language reflects your lack of vision and direction. If, on the other hand, you have a clear goal which you can *(and do)* articulate fairly often — even if only to yourself — you stand an excellent chance of reaching that goal.

The same, of course, holds true if you have your own business. Do you use language that is consistent with the growth of your business? Or do you constantly talk about how you'll never get to the next level?

4. Health

Without question, our words have a profound impact on our health. For example, imagine that a group of us sat down to what seemed to be a perfectly wholesome and delicious meal. Then, two hours later I called and told you that every person who ate with us had been rushed to the hospital and treated for food poisoning! Suppose that you felt perfectly fine before I called. How would you react after hearing my information?

Most likely, you'd clutch your stomach, get pale and feel very ill. Why? Because my words instilled a belief in you which, in turn, your body started acting upon. This same bodily reaction would have occurred even if I was playing a cruel joke and was lying about the whole situation! Your body responds to words it hears you and other people say. That's why it makes absolutely no sense to keep repeating that you have "chronic back pain that will *never* go away" or that you get "three or four bad colds *every* year." By uttering these statements, you are actually instructing your body to manifest pain and disease!

Please don't misunderstand. I'm not suggesting that you deny pain or disease — or that you can overcome *any* illness — but there's certainly nothing to be gained (and much harm that can flow) from using language that reinforces suffering and incurability.

You Have A Choice

Well, have you thought about the words you use in these four areas of your life? When we repeat certain phrases over and over, it's as if a "groove" is formed in our brain. We keep replaying the same old refrain in our heads like a broken record. The trouble is, whenever you say these words you just deepen the groove, replaying the same old myths in your mind, strengthening the same old beliefs… and getting the same old results.

Recognize, however, that just because you've said things in the past there's no reason to blindly continue doing so. While it takes some discipline and vigilance on your part to make changes in your language, it's well worth the effort! So, from now on, consciously *choose* words that will point you in the direction of your goals. Ask a friend to remind you when you slip.

Remember, it's up to you to speak in a way that will move you toward what you want in life. Therefore, use words that are consistent with the path you truly wish to be on… take action along those lines… and watch yourself begin to travel in that wonderful direction!

LESSON 7 ————————————

How Are You?

Your day goes the way the corners of your mouth turn.

— Unknown

Our answer to the question *How are you?* seems like such a small thing. But we must answer that question at least 10 times a day — and perhaps as many as 50. So it's not a small thing at all. It's a significant part of our daily conversations.

When someone asks *How are you?* what do you say? Your answer is usually no more than a few words. And yet, that short response tells a lot about you — and your attitude. In fact, your response can literally shape your attitude.

I've observed that the responses to *How are you?* can be classified into three categories: negative, mediocre and positive. Let's examine these three categories and some common responses under each one.

Negative Responses

The negative replies to *How are you?* include phrases such as:

"Lousy."

"Terrible."

"I'm tired."

"It's not my day."

"Thank God it's Friday."

"A day older and a dollar broker."

"Don't ask."

When someone responds with "Don't ask," I know I'm in for trouble. That person is going to unleash a multitude of complaints and make me sorry for asking *How are you?* in the first place!

And I really pity those who take the "Thank God it's Friday" approach to life. Think of what they're saying. "Monday, Tuesday, Wednesday and Thursday are bad days every week." For these people, four-fifths of their work week is lousy! The fifth day, Friday, is "bearable" only because they know they'll have the next two days off! Is this a way to live your life? Are you beginning to see how these negative phrases can poison your attitude... and turn off other people?

Mediocre Responses

Those in the mediocre group are a step up from the negative bunch — but they still have plenty of room for improvement. Here are some of the things they say:

"I'm okay."

"Not too bad."

"Could be worse."

"Same old, same old."

"Hangin' in there."

"Fine."

Do you really want to spend a lot of time with someone who thinks that life is "not too bad"? Is that the person you want to do business with? When we use words like these, we also diminish our energy. Can you imagine someone saying "Could be worse" with an upright posture... and a lot of enthusiasm? Of course not. These people sound like they haven't slept in two days.

There's no getting around it. People who use mediocre words will develop a mediocre attitude... and get mediocre results. And I know you don't want that!

Positive Responses

Then, there's the positive approach. These are the enthusiastic people who say:

"Terrific."

"Fantastic."

"Great."

"Excellent."

"Super."

"I'm on top of the world."

"It doesn't get any better."

Those who use positive words like these have a bounce in their step and *you* feel a little better just by being around them. Be honest. How did you feel as you read the positive list? I don't know about you, but I'm energized and excited as I review that list. These are the people I look forward to meeting today. These are the people who are more likely to get my business.

Why not go back and re-read the negative list and the mediocre list. Say them out loud. How do they make you feel? Bummed out, for sure!

A smile is an inexpensive way to improve your looks.
— Unknown

You see, if given the choice, I'd rather be around people who are positive and full of life... as opposed to those who are negative and listless. It's like the old saying that everybody lights up a room — *some when they walk into the room... and some when they walk out!* You want to be the one who lights up a room when you walk in!

As for me, when someone asks me *How are you?* I usually respond with *Terrific!* It projects a positive attitude to the other person and the more I say it, the more I feel terrific!

Join The Positive Group

Well, you've had a chance to review some typical responses in each category — negative, mediocre and positive. Which of these phrases do you use most often? Which responses do your friends and family use?

If you find yourself in the negative or mediocre group, I suggest you immediately consider revising your response and joining the ranks of the positive. Here's why. When you're asked *How are you?* and you say *Horrible or Not too bad*, your physiology is adversely affected. You tend to slump your shoulders and head and take on a depressed posture.

What about your emotions? After stating that you're *lousy*, do you feel better? Of course not. You feel even more down in the dumps because negative words and thoughts generate negative feelings, and eventually, negative results.

And it's up to you to break it. Even if real circumstances in your life persuaded you to state that you're *lousy* — perhaps a promising business deal fell through, or your child received poor grades in school — your gloomy attitude does nothing to improve the situation. To make matters worse, your mediocre or negative reply turns others off; they're dragged down just being around you and hearing your pessimism.

Form A New Habit

If all of these negative consequences flow from your words, why do you continue to say them? More than likely, it's because you haven't recognized that you have a *choice* in the matter. Instead, you're following a habit that you developed many years ago... a habit that no longer serves you.

In the end, your own words are a self-fulfilling prophesy — if you say *Everything is terrible*, your mind is attracted to those people and circumstances that will cause that statement to be true. If, on the other hand, you repeatedly state that your life is *Wonderful!* your mind will begin to move you in a positive direction.

For instance, just consider what happens when you respond that you're *Excellent!* or *Terrific!* As you say these words, your physiology begins to correspond with your optimistic language. Your posture is more upright. Other people are attracted to your energy and vitality. Your business and personal relationships improve. Will all of your life's problems magically disappear? No, but you've set in motion a very important principle: *We get what we expect in life.*

I can tell you from firsthand experience that this is one of those little things in life that makes a big difference. About 25 years ago, when someone asked me *How are you?* I'd say something like *Okay* with very little energy. You know what I was doing? I was programming myself to have "okay" relationships with people. I was programming myself to have "okay" success. I was programming myself to have an "okay" attitude... and an "okay" life.

> *Say you are well,*
> *or all is well with you,*
> *and God shall hear your*
> *words and make them*
> *come true.*
>
> — *Ella Wheeler Wilcox*

But then, thank goodness, I learned that I didn't have to settle for an "okay" life! So I picked up my response a few notches and began to say *Terrific!* I said it with some energy. Sure, at first it was a little uncomfortable. Some people looked at me like I was a little strange. But after about a week, it started to come naturally to me. And I was amazed at how much better I felt, and how people were much more interested in talking with me.

Believe me, this is not rocket science. You don't need talent, money or good looks to have a great attitude You just need to get in the habit of using a high-energy, positive response, and you'll get the same exciting results I got!

What If I Don't Feel Terrific?

Whenever I do a presentation and recommend to the audience that they give a very upbeat response to *How are you?* someone always comes up to me afterward and says, "What if I really don't feel terrific? I don't want to lie to my friends and co-workers by telling them everything is wonderful when it isn't."

Now don't get me wrong. I put the highest value on integrity... and telling the truth. Yet, I don't think this is a matter of telling the truth. Let me explain.

Assume for a moment that Sally feels tired. When someone at work asks her *How are you?* she wants to be perfectly honest so she says, *I'm tired.* Here's what will happen. Sally will reinforce the belief that she's tired. She'll feel even more fatigued. She'll probably slump her shoulders and let out a sigh. She'll have a lousy, unproductive day at work.

And let's get back to the person who asked Sally the question — and who probably regrets it now! That person also feels worse. After all, when someone tells you how tired she is, do you feel uplifted? No way. Just the suggestion of the word "tired" and you start yawning. So, Sally has brought herself down, as well as her co-worker.

Okay, Sally goes home after her grueling day, and now she's exhausted. So she plops into her favorite chair and opens the newspaper to look at the winning lottery numbers. As she pulls her own ticket out of her wallet, she discovers that she's holding the winning ticket. She just won $10 million!

A cloudy day is no match for a sunny disposition.
— William Arthur Ward

What do you think Sally would do? Remember, she's *very* tired.

You and I both know that Sally would leap out of her chair, be jumping up and down, screaming and waving her arms in the air. You'd think she was leading an aerobics class. Naturally, she'd run to pick up the phone to call her family and friends. She'd be a bundle of energy and would probably stay up all night celebrating... and planning what to do with the money!

But wait a second. Ten seconds ago, this woman was exhausted. Now, she's got the energy of a 15-year-old cheerleader who has just been told she made the cheerleading squad. What happened in those 10 seconds to change someone from being utterly exhausted… to wildly exuberant? Did she get a shot of vitamin B-12? Did anyone throw a bucket of ice water in her face?

No. Her transformation was entirely mental!

Now I'm not trying to diminish what Sally was feeling. Her fatigue was very real, but it wasn't as much physical as mental. So, was Sally telling the truth when she said she was tired? It really has very little to do with the truth. It's a matter of what Sally *chose* to focus on. She could concentrate on feeling tired. That was one option. On the other hand, she could have thought about the many blessings in her life and felt very fortunate and energized.

How we feel is very often a subjective matter. When we tell ourselves that we're tired, we feel tired. When we tell ourselves that we feel terrific, we feel energized. As you'll recall from Lesson 2, we become what we think about.

Respond With Enthusiasm

For the next month, try this experiment. When anyone asks *How are you?* — whether it's someone at work or a cashier at the store — respond with energy and enthusiasm that you're *Great!* or *Terrific!* Say it with a smile and a sparkle in your eye. It doesn't matter whether or not you completely and totally *feel* terrific at that moment. Simply apply the *act-as-if* principle. In other words, if you want to be more positive, act-as-if you already are and, pretty soon, you'll find that you have, in fact, become more positive!

Don't worry if you feel a little uncomfortable saying these words at the beginning. Stick with it and eventually you'll grow into it. You'll quickly notice that you feel better… that others want to be around you… and that positive results will come your way.

By the way, *How are you?*

I can almost hear you say T-E-R-R-I-F-I-C!

LESSON 8

Stop Complaining!

Troubles, like babies, grow larger by nursing.
— Lady Holland

How do you feel when someone unloads all of his problems and complaints on you? Not very uplifting and energizing, is it? The truth is, nobody likes to be around a complainer — except, perhaps, other complainers.

Of course, all of us complain at one time or another. The important question is: How *often* do you complain? If you're wondering whether you complain too much, simply ask your friends, relatives or co-workers. They'll let you know.

Now, when I say "complain," I'm not talking about those instances when you discuss your problems in an attempt to search for solutions. That's constructive and commendable. And I'm not referring to those occasions when you share your life experiences (including disappointments) with friends or relatives in the context of bringing them up to date on the latest developments in your life. After all, part of being human is sharing our experiences and supporting each other.

Nobody Wants To Hear About Your Aches And Pains

Maybe a few examples will give you a better idea about the kind of complaining that's counterproductive. One of the most common areas of complaint is the subject of illness. In this category are comments such as "My back is killing me" or "I have a terrible sinus headache." Worse yet, some people get very graphic in explaining the gory details of their particular ailment (such as "I had this green stuff oozing out of my...") And doesn't it just make your day when your co-worker tells you that he or she is nauseous?

Let's face it. What can I possibly do for you if you have a stomach ache? I'm not a physician — go to a doctor if you have a medical problem. More importantly, *why* are you telling *me* this? You might want sympathy, but all you're doing is dragging me down and reinforcing your own suffering. Talking about pain and discomfort will only bring you more of the same — and encourage those around you to look for the exits.

Self-pity is an acid which eats holes in happiness.

— Earl Nightingale

When it comes to complaints about illness, the *principle of escalation* usually rears its ugly head. Here's how it works. You tell your friend about the agony you went through with the flu. Your friend interrupts and says, "You think *you* had it bad. When *I* had the flu, I had a 104 degree fever and had to be rushed to the hospital. I almost died." Or, tell someone that your back or foot hurts — and count how many *seconds* it takes for that person to switch the conversation to his or her own back pain and aching feet. Complainers love to play this game — their pain is always worse than yours.

Don't Let It Rain On Your Parade

Another favorite complaint area is the weather. It starts to rain and people say, "What a lousy, miserable day." Why does some moisture from the heavens make it a lousy day? When someone makes that remark to me, I respond, "It's wet out — but it's a *great* day!" By associating rain with "lousy day," you're programming yourself in a negative way. Furthermore, your complaints about the weather won't change the conditions. It simply makes no sense to get upset about things over which you have no control — and which have no significant impact on your life.

Finally, there are the petty complaints, such as "The waiter didn't come over to take my order for five minutes" or "John got an office with a larger window than I have." Life presents too many difficult challenges for us to get bogged down with silly things like that. And when you gripe about insignificant things, you're also saying something about yourself. If I'm your employer or a member of your team, I'm wondering how you'll react when we *really* have a problem worth worrying about!

He Had Every Reason To Complain

Several years ago I was in my office and thinking about some of the things that weren't going as well as I had planned. You know, the typical business problems — results not happening as fast as I had expected. And I'll confess that I'd been doing a little complaining about it.

Then Pedro walked in. Pedro is in his early 20s and came to this country about six years ago from Honduras. He works for a company that cleans homes and offices. You talk about a positive attitude! Pedro is one of the most positive people I've ever met — always smiling and upbeat.

On this day, however, I asked Pedro about Hurricane Mitch and its impact on his homeland. The smile quickly left his face. He told me of the devastation the hurricane had caused. Thousands of people had died. More than a million people were left homeless.

Pedro said that his father, mother and brother still lived in Honduras, and he had no idea if they were dead or alive.

He had no way to contact them — all the phone lines in that area had been destroyed. Pedro said he thought about his family every day.

Can you imagine the agony of not even knowing if your family is still alive?

Then Pedro went on to tell me about all the things he was doing to help the people in Honduras. He was collecting money, clothing and other necessities. He was actively working with the relief organizations. Instead of just griping about the problem, he was doing whatever he could do to ease their pain.

> *The secret of happiness is to count your blessings while others are adding up their troubles.*
>
> — William Penn

After speaking with Pedro, I began to realize just how inconsequential my own problems were... and how fortunate I am! You better believe I stopped complaining. I faced the rest of the day with renewed energy and a much better attitude.

By the way, several weeks later I saw Pedro again. And yes, he had his usual winning smile and his great attitude. The good news is that his family members survived. The bad news is that they lost everything in the flood and had to live in a shelter temporarily. Clean water was very scarce after the flood. Disease was rampant. I can't even fathom what it's like to lose everything you own and have to start over from scratch, especially under these difficult conditions. Can you?

There's no doubt about it. Pedro has every reason to whine about his family's bad luck. But he doesn't. He realizes that complaining would be a terrible waste of his time and energy. Thank you, Pedro for reminding all of us that complaining is not the answer to our challenges in life.

Putting Things In Perspective

There's another valuable lesson that we can learn from Pedro — and that's the importance of keeping things in perspective.   Over the years, I've noticed that complainers lack perspective — they tend to blow their problems way out of proportion.

Optimistic people... people with great attitudes... tend to have a sense of what's truly important in life.

The dictionary defines perspective as "the capacity to view things in their true relation or relative importance."   Think about the people you know. Do you have any friends who get bent out of shape because they got a flat tire? And how about those who sever ties with close family members because of a dispute over the seating arrangements at a wedding? It's clear these folks have lost sight of the "relative importance" of things!

> *Reflect upon your present blessings, of which every man has plenty; not on your past misfortunes, of which all men have some.*
>
> — Charles Dickens

I think we can all learn from Eddie Rickenbacker, who drifted in a life raft for 21 days, hopelessly lost in the Pacific. After surviving the ordeal, Rickenbacker said, *"If you have all the fresh water you want to drink and all the food you want to eat, you ought never complain about anything."*

Let me share with you some of the things I'm grateful for:

1. I'm in good health.
2. Dolores is in good health.
3. We have our own home.
4. We have plenty of food to eat and clean water to drink.
5. We live in the United States and enjoy freedom.
6. I love my work.
7. I get to travel and meet fascinating people.
8. I have many loyal friends.
9. I draw strength from my relationship with God.

This is just a partial list of the blessings in my life. And you know what? Even with all of these wonderful things, there are times when I start to take some of them for granted! But I've learned to quickly re-connect with these blessings… and it boosts my attitude and brings me right back on course.

So, what is it that you've been complaining about lately? Are they really "life and death" matters? The next time you're tempted to gripe about your problems, pick up a pen and piece of paper and start listing all the reasons you have to be grateful!

Let me tell you, it sure beats complaining!

If you're all wrapped up in yourself, you're overdressed.

— Kate Halverson

Be A Source Of Positive News

I'm not suggesting that you just sit back and ignore all of the problems in your life. However, rather than complaining, it's far better to focus your attention and your energy on those steps you can take to solve, or at least lessen, your problem. For instance, let's say you're feeling a little tired lately. Instead of telling everyone how lousy you feel, make an effort to exercise more regularly or get to bed a little earlier.

To review: Complaints work against you in three ways. First, no one wants to hear negative news about your illness and your problems. Second, complaining reinforces your own pain and discomfort. So why keep replaying painful, negative memories? Third, complaining, by itself, accomplishes nothing and diverts you from the constructive actions you could be taking to improve your situation.

It's been said that 90 percent of the people don't care about your problems… and the other 10 percent are glad you have them! Seriously though, all of us can cut down on our complaining. From now on, let's do ourselves and others a favor and make our conversations uplifting.

The people who don't complain very much (and those who speak *positively*) are a joy to be around. Decide to join that group — so people won't have to cross the street when they see you coming!

PART 3

Heaven Helps
Those Who Act

Nothing happens by itself. It all will come your way once you understand that you have to make it come your way, by your own exertions.

— Ben Stein

LESSON 9

Associate with Positive People

A mirror reflects a man's face, but what he is really like is shown by the kind of friends he chooses.
— The Living Bible, Proverbs 27

In high school, Mike spent a lot of time with a bunch of guys in his neighborhood. According to Mike, these guys just liked to sit on the front porch and watch cars go by. They had no goals and no dreams. They were always negative.

Whenever Mike suggested they do something new, the others would discourage him. "It's stupid" or "not cool," they told him. Mike just went along with them, so he could remain part of the group.

When Mike went off to college, he still ran into some negative people. But he also met people who were positive... who wanted to learn... who wanted to achieve things. Mike decided to spend his time with the positive people. Almost immediately, Mike started to feel much better about himself. He developed a great attitude. He began to set goals.

And I'm happy to tell you Mike now runs his own successful video production company and has a wonderful family. One by one, he is accomplishing all of the goals he has set. When I asked Mike what happened to his high school friends, he told me, "They still live in the same neighborhood. They're still negative. And they're still doing nothing with their lives!"

Mike added, *"I'd never be where I am now if I kept hanging out with those guys. I'd still be at the corner deli playing pinball."*

Mike's story is a great reminder about the influence others have on our lives. And yet sometimes we get in the habit of being with certain people — and we just don't think about the consequences.

Have you ever heard the axiom *"Tell me who you hang out with and I'll tell you who you are"*? There's a lot of wisdom in that simple statement. Have you given much thought to how this principle has been molding and shaping your life?

Think back to when you were growing up. Do you remember how concerned our parents were about who we hung out with? Our mom or dad wanted to meet our friends and know all kinds of details about them. Why? Our parents knew that we'd be greatly influenced by our friends... that we'd tend to pick up some of their habits... and that we'd probably do the things our friends were doing. Our parents were concerned for good reason. And I'll bet that if you have children, you closely watch their friends — because of the impact these youngsters will have on your children.

Toxic People And Nourishing People

In today's literature, we see the terms *toxic* people and *nourishing* people. As you might expect, toxic people are the ones who always dwell on the negative. The dictionary defines toxic as "poisonous"; toxic people continually spew their verbal poison. In contrast, the dictionary definition of nourishing is "to promote the growth of." Nourishing people are positive and supportive. They lift your spirits and are a joy to be around.

Toxic people will always try to drag you down to their level. They hammer away at you with all of the things you can't do and all of the things that are impossible. They barrage you with gloomy statements about the lousy economy, the problems in their life, the problems soon to be in your life and the terrible prospects for the future. If you're lucky, they might even throw in a few words about their aches and pains.

> *We become part of what we are around.*
> — Unknown

After listening to toxic people, you feel listless and drained. Motivational speaker Les Brown refers to these people as "Dream Killers." Psychologist Jack Canfield describes them as "energy vampires" because they suck all the positive energy out of you. Have you ever been with a negative person — and felt as if that individual were physically taking energy from you? I think we've all had that experience many times. One thing is certain: Spend time with toxic people and their negative messages will wear you down.

On the other hand, how do you feel when you're around people who are positive, enthusiastic and supportive? You're energized and inspired. There's something truly amazing about positive people. They seem to have a positive energy that lights up a room. When you're around them, you start to pick up their attitude and you feel as if you have added strength to vigorously pursue your own goals.

When I think about positive people, my friend John Lisicich immediately comes to mind. Whenever I speak with John, I feel like I can conquer the world. John is simply the most positive person you could ever meet.

I like to think of myself as a very positive person. On a scale of 1-10, with 10 being the most positive, I'd probably give myself a 9.5. I'd have to give John Lisicich a 14! He's just off the charts. He's always positive, always enthusiastic. And he gives a tremendous lift to everyone who crosses his path. His attitude inspires people to greatness!

Can you see how your attitude might improve if you had a friend like John in your life?

Those Silly Songs On The Radio

I'm sure it has happened to you many times. You hear a song on the radio, and you say to yourself, "What a ridiculous song." Later that day, you hear the same song again. The following day, you hear that song a few more times. As the song climbs the charts, you can't get away from it. You hear it several times each day for a week.

Then something incredible happens. You're sitting at home and all of a sudden, you start to hum or sing that silly song! If, at that very moment, I were to ask you what you think of the song, you'd tell me, "It's horrible." Then why on earth are you singing it? The reality is, whatever you hear over and over will be at the forefront of your consciousness.

As you also know, once that song becomes less popular... and isn't played as frequently on the radio... you'll tend to think about it (and sing it to yourself!) much less often. There's an important lesson here. The mind tends to dwell upon whatever is repeated over and over. Unfortunately, the mind doesn't discriminate between messages that are good for us and those that are harmful. If we hear something often enough, we will tend to believe it... and act upon it. Just as a song repeated many times will get us thinking about that song, so too will repeated thoughts about success get us thinking about success!

Your friends will stretch your vision... or choke your dreams.

— Unknown

So if we'll make sure to fill our mind with positive messages, we're going to be more positive and move forward boldly to achieve our goals. The more positive reinforcement the better. And where can we get this positive reinforcement? Well, one way is to read motivational books.

Congratulations... because you're doing that right now! In addition, we can listen to motivational audio programs — and spend lots of time with positive people.

Smokey's Sponge Theory

I've learned a lot about attitude and the importance of surrounding myself with positive people from my friend Glen "Smokey" Stover. Smokey worked in sales for 45 years in the cemetery and funeral home industry. While this may sound like a gloomy field, let me assure you that Smokey is a positive dynamo! Every time I get off the phone with Smokey, I feel terrific.

Smokey explained to me that human beings are like sponges: We "soak up" whatever people around us are saying. So, if we spend time with someone who's negative, we sponge up the negatives and it affects our attitude. Of course, the reverse is also true. When we hang around positive people we soak up the positive. We feel better... and perform better.

I once asked Smokey, "What do you do if you're speaking with a negative person?"

He said, "I get away from that person as soon as I can. I'll say something like, 'Gosh, it's been good to see you, Charlie,' and I move on to another person."

Then I asked Smokey, "Did you ever have a friend who was negative?"

"Not for very long," he said.

Well put, Smokey!

Evaluate Your Friendships

It's crucial that you evaluate your friendships from time to time — even those you've maintained for many years. Trust me, this isn't a minor issue. Those who occupy your time have a significant impact on your most priceless possession — *your mind!*

Are you surrounding yourself with negative friends and spending a lot of time with them in your leisure hours? If so, I'm going to ask you to think about spending much less time with these people — or even no time at all with them.

Sounds harsh, doesn't it? After all, I'm suggesting that you limit — or eliminate — your involvement with some long-standing friends. When I tell people this at my seminars, invariably someone will raise a hand and accuse me of being cold or uncaring. The audience member will typically say, "Shouldn't we try to help our negative friends instead of dumping them?"

Well, you're free to do whatever you think is best, and each situation must be dealt with on its own unique facts. However, I've found that in most cases, hanging around these negative friends doesn't help them — and it doesn't help you, either! Everyone gets dragged down because most negative people don't want to change. They just want someone to listen to their tales of woe.

> *Are the things around you helping you toward success — or are they holding you back?*
>
> — W. Clement Stone

If you have a strong urge to spend time with negative friends, ask yourself: "Why am I choosing to be with these people?" Consciously or unconsciously, you may be choosing to hold yourself back — to be less than you are capable of becoming.

By the way, I think it's wonderful to try to help someone overcome their negativity. But if you've been trying for several years... and aren't getting anywhere... maybe it's time to move on!

Let me clarify one important point. I'm not making a judgment here that negative people are any less worthy than other people. I'm saying there are consequences if you spend time with people who are negative. What are the consequences? You'll be less happy and less successful than you could be.

Toxic Relatives

What do you do if you happen to have toxic relatives? Obviously, this is a touchy issue. What I'm going to suggest is that you don't turn your back on your family members. Family ties are precious, and I think we must make every effort to maintain harmonious family relationships.

Even so, I recommend that you put some controls in place that reduce the impact your toxic relatives have on your life. You're not abandoning them or refusing to speak with them, but you *are* putting some limits on your involvement with them.

For example, if you have negative relatives, I suggest that you don't go out of your way to call them on the phone several times each day if you know they're going to put you down or criticize your every move. What good can possibly come from that? We get bombarded with enough negativity as it is — just turn on the radio or TV or read a newspaper. Do we need our relatives to provide even more negative news? I don't think so!

And here's another suggestion that will work equally well whether you're talking with a friend or a relative. When the discussion moves to a negative subject, resist the temptation to accuse the other person of being negative. That will usually makes things even worse. Instead, gently shift the conversation to a more positive topic.

Remember that I'm not asking you to disown your relatives or refuse to attend family functions. This is about limiting your contacts with negative relatives so you don't get dragged down to their level!

Positive People In The Workplace

Just about every organization has some negative people working there. And sometimes you have to interact and work alongside these people. But don't go out of your way to spend time with these prophets of gloom and doom.

For instance, if you frequently have lunch with negative people at work, stop having lunch with them! All they're doing is filling your mind with negativity. You can't perform at your best if you allow these people to dump their negative garbage into your mind. There's no need to be nasty or to tell them off. You should be able to find a diplomatic way of distancing yourself from this "poisonous" group.

> *Good friends are good for your health.*
> — Dr. Irwin Sarason

Instead, take charge. Be proactive. Make it a point to eat at your desk... to take a client out to lunch... or to sit at a different table in the cafeteria. Do whatever you have to do to make lunch a *positive* experience.

Make no mistake about it. Positive people are welcomed in any organization... and negative people are hurting their chances for advancement. The problem of negative workers has gotten so bad that I recently got a brochure in the mail announcing a full-day seminar entitled *"How To Legally Fire Employees With Attitude Problems!"*

The business community is waking up to the fact that when it comes to productivity in the workplace, *attitude is everything!*

Choose Your Friends Wisely

As I said at the beginning of this lesson, *"Tell me who you hang out with and I'll tell you who you are."* If you're serious about getting a raise or a promotion at work... succeeding in your own business... or improving yourself as a human being, then you have to start associating with people who can take you to the next level.

As you increase your associations with nourishing people, you'll feel better about yourself and have renewed energy to achieve your goals. You'll become a more positive, upbeat person — the kind of person others love to be around. I used to think it was *important* to associate with positive people and to limit involvement with negative people. Now, I believe it's *essential* if you want to be a high achiever and a happy individual.

So, surround yourself with positive, nourishing people — they'll lift you up the ladder of success.

LESSON 10 ⎯⎯⎯⎯⎯⎯

Confront Your Fears and Grow

> *Do the thing you fear and the death of fear is certain.*
>
> —Ralph Waldo Emerson

As I sat in the audience listening to motivational speaker Gil Eagles, little did I know that one sentence was about to change my life.

Gil Eagles gave a marvelous presentation that day. He had many valuable things to say. But there was one line — one absolute gem — that stands out. Here's what he said:

"If you want to be successful, you must be willing to be uncomfortable."

I'll never forget those words. And Gil was right on the money. To achieve your goals and realize your potential, you must be willing to be *uncomfortable* — to do things that you're afraid to do. That's how you develop your potential!

Sounds so simple, doesn't it? And yet, what do most people do when they face a frightening situation or new activity? They back away from the fear. They don't take action. I know... because that's what I did for the first 30 years of my life. And I can tell you without hesitation that it's a losing strategy.

Show me a successful person and I'll show you someone who confronts his or her fears and takes action!

Examining Our Fears

Have *you* ever been afraid or anxious before trying a new or challenging activity? Has that fear ever stopped you from taking action? I'm sure you've been paralyzed by fear at one time or another in your life. I know I have. That's simply part of being human.

Of course, every person has a different fear threshold. What frightens one person to death might have little impact on someone else. For example, to some, speaking in public or starting a new business is scary. Others might be fearful about asking someone for directions... or for a date. Regardless of how trivial or silly you believe your fears may be, this lesson applies to you.

Nothing in life is to be feared. It is only to be understood.

— Marie Curie

When I talk about fear, I'm *not* referring to physical risks that might injure you or endanger your health, such as diving off cliffs in Acapulco or bungee jumping. I'm scared of those things, too — and I have no plans to do either of them. What I'm talking about here are those challenges that stand in the way of your personal and professional growth. These are the things that scare you — but which you know are necessary if you're going to get what you want in life.

The Comfort Zone

When you're gripped by fear and anxiety, it's usually because you're stepping out of your *comfort zone*. Let's take some time to discuss this important concept — and how it relates to your success and the development of your potential.

Each of us has a comfort zone, a zone of behavior that

is familiar to us and where we feel comfortable and safe.
Think of your comfort zone as the inside of a circle.

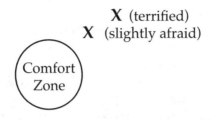

X (terrified)
X (slightly afraid)

Comfort
Zone

The activities and situations that lie inside the circle are
non-threatening and familiar. They're routine, part of your
everyday life — the things you can do with no sweat. In
this category are tasks such as speaking to your friends or
co-workers or filling out the daily paperwork at your job.

However, you occasionally face experiences or challenges that are *outside* your comfort zone. These are represented
by the "Xs" in the diagram above. The farther the "X" is
from the circle, the more afraid you are to participate in that
activity.

When faced with something outside your comfort zone,
you suddenly feel nervous. Your palms become sweaty and
your heart pounds. You begin to wonder,

"Will I be able to handle it?

"Will others laugh at me?

"What will my friends and relatives say?"

As you look at the diagram above, what does the "X"
represent for you? In other words, what fear is holding you
back from reaching the next level of success or fulfillment
in your life?

Is it fear of approaching new prospects?

Is it fear about changing careers?

Is it fear about learning new skills?

Is it fear of going back to school?

Is it fear of telling other people what's on your mind?

Is it fear of public speaking?

Whatever that "X" represents for you, just be honest
and admit it. My guess is that thousands, if not millions, of

people have the very same fear you have! In fact, let's take a closer look at what most people are afraid of.

The Most Common Fears

During many of my presentations, I distribute index cards to the audience members and ask them to write down, anonymously, the fears that are standing in the way of their professional and personal growth. Then, I collect the cards and read them aloud.

What do you think people write on those index cards? In most audiences, regardless of profession or geographical location, the same answers come up again and again. Here are some of the most common fears they identify:

1. *Public Speaking or Giving Presentations.* In virtually every group, this is the #1 fear. The vast majority of people are terrified about speaking in front of a group of people.

2. *Hearing the word "NO" or having their ideas rejected.* This response is very common among salespeople, especially those who make cold calls.

3. *Changing Jobs or Starting Their Own Business.* Over the years, I've noticed that more and more people are listing this fear. We have a lot of unhappy workers in corporate America today, and they yearn for a more satisfying work environment... but they're afraid to do anything about it!

4. *Telling Managers or Executives "Negative News" (what the managers or executives don't want to hear).* This one is self-explanatory.

5. *Talking to People in Upper Management.* Many entry-level workers and even managers are terrified about speaking to executives in the company. They even hesitate to make "small talk" with the president

or CEO of their organization — for fear they'll say something silly or appear stupid.

6. *Fear of Failure.* Those who won't try something new for fear that it won't work out. (We'll tackle this issue in more depth in Lesson 11.)

Well, are you surprised by any of the fears on this list? Do you have any of them now — or have you had them in the past? The truth is, the overwhelming majority of people experience these fears at some point in their lives.

And if you have some fears that weren't on this list, don't worry about it. You are stronger than any of your fears... and you *can* overcome them!

The "Benefit" Of Backing Away From Your Fears

When confronted with an anxiety-producing event, most people will retreat to avoid the fear and anxiety. That's what I used to do. You see, backing away *does* relieve the fear and anxiety that would have resulted if you followed through with the activity. For instance, if someone asks you to make a presentation within your company, and you decline, you save yourself the sleepless nights you'd have worrying about it... and the nervousness you'd experience in the days leading up to the presentation.

In fact, I've found that's the one and only benefit you get by retreating — a momentary avoidance of anxiety.

Think about it for a moment. Can you list any other benefits that people get when they refuse to confront their fears? I've asked that question of thousands of people, and nobody has been able to come up with any additional benefits. For good reason — there are none!

The Price You Pay

Now, I want you to seriously consider the price you pay when you back away from those fears that are standing in the way of your growth. Here's what happens:

Your self-esteem is lowered.
You feel powerless and frustrated.

You sabotage your success.
You lead an uneventful, boring life.

Is this a price worth paying for the short-term avoidance of fear and anxiety? Most of us are indeed willing to pay this dear price, simply to avoid temporary discomfort and possible ridicule from others.

Trust me folks, this is insane! In the long run, retreating is not the best way to handle your problem. You'll never be highly successful or develop your talents to the fullest unless you're willing to confront your fears.

My High School Strategy

When I was in high school, I was pretty shy and didn't feel very good about myself. But I was never rejected when it came to asking someone for a date. If you were looking at me now, you'd probably be thinking, "He's not bad looking, but he's certainly no Tom Cruise."

My strategy was really quite simple. *I never asked anyone out on a date.* You see, I wasn't going to let anyone reject me. And what did I accomplish? I felt horrible about myself. I knew that I had "wimped out." I felt powerless, and as you can imagine, I didn't have a full social calendar. I was sabotaging my success!

> *He who loses wealth loses much; he who loses a friend loses more; but he who loses courage loses all.*
>
> — Miguel de Cervantes

Because I refused to face my fear, I remained in the background while most of my friends and class-mates went out on dates. How do you think that made me feel? *Pretty lousy*, just as you'd expect. In case you're wondering, I did have a few dates during that period of my life, but only when other people arranged them. I wasn't going to allow anyone to say "NO" to me. In reality I was saying "NO" to myself.

Can you see how my strategy of backing away from my fears worked against me? Now it's true that if I had asked some people for a date in high school, a few of them might have said "NO." But you know what? I wouldn't have died! I could have asked another person... and another... and eventually I would have gotten a "YES."

It wasn't until college that I began to take some "baby steps" to confront this fear of rejection. Little by little, I gained more confidence. And in law school, I had the good fortune to meet Dolores, and we've been married going on 30 years!

A New Life

I'm really no different from you. I have my fears, just as you do. And when I look back at the first 30 years of my life, you know what I see? I see someone who achieved some degree of success as an attorney. But I also see someone who was shy, insecure, scared and self-conscious. Does that sound to you like someone who's a motivational speaker?

What turned my life around... and improved it a million-fold... is that I learned to confront my fears and take action. I realized after years of frustration and disappointments that hiding from my fears wasn't getting me anywhere — and it would *never* get me anywhere.

Of course, I wouldn't have confronted my fears if I hadn't first developed a positive attitude. A "can-do" attitude provided me with the extra push I needed to take action. When you believe you can do something, you have the courage to move forward despite being afraid.

Armed with a great attitude, I decided to become a participant in life and to explore my potential, even though I was scared. From the very beginning, I felt so much better about myself. I had taken control of my life, and all sorts of possibilities opened up for me.

Are you beginning to see the incredible rewards you can receive when you're willing to develop a positive attitude and confront your fears?

Reframe The Situation

If I could give you a way to confront uncomfortable situations without fear or anxiety, you'd be ecstatic and eternally grateful, wouldn't you? Sorry, but there's no such magical solution. I can't wave a magic wand and take away your fears.

How then can you muster the courage to do those things that you fear, but which are necessary for your success and growth?

The next time you face a scary situation, I suggest you take a different outlook. Most people start thinking, "I won't be able to do this well and other people may laugh at me or reject me." They get hung up about how well they're going to perform. Because of these worries, they decide to retreat. While you should always go in with a positive attitude and prepare beforehand to the extent possible, don't be *overly* concerned with the result.

Consider yourself an immediate winner when you take the step and do the thing you fear. That's right. You're a winner just by entering the arena and participating, regardless of the result.

Moving Forward Even When You're Afraid

For instance, let's assume you're afraid to speak in public, but you confront your fear and do it anyway. The moment you get up and speak before the audience, you're a winner. Your knees may be shaking and your voice may be quivering. That doesn't matter. You faced your fear and accepted the challenge. Congratulations are in order. The likely result is that your self-esteem will be enhanced and you'll feel exhilarated.

On your first attempt, you won't be hailed as the world's finest speaker. So what? Let's face it. You can't expect to be an accomplished speaker during your first presentation. Were you a great tennis player after your first game? Or a great swimmer the first time you entered the water? Developing any skill takes time.

I remember *my* first motivational speech. That was in 1988... and my performance was nothing to write home about! I gave a free talk to a group of real estate salespeople, and let me tell you, I was terrified. I couldn't take my eyes off my notes. Fortunately, the content of my presentation was very solid and the audience responded well. But I had a long way to go before I could call myself a good speaker.

On the second presentation, I was a little better. And when I had done five or so presentations, I began to rely less and less on my notes… and to develop a stronger connection with the audience. Now, 20 years later, I'm a professional speaker who speaks to thousands of people each year throughout the United States and abroad.

But let's not forget that it all started with a scared guy who gave a very unimpressive talk in 1988.

She Followed Her Dream

I'd like to tell you a story about a woman who knows a lot about breaking out of a comfort zone. Her name is Dottie Burman, and for 32 years Dottie was a high school English teacher in New York. Yet, since the age of 10, she wanted to go into show business. She never gave it serious thought as a career and instead chose the security of teaching, with its regular paycheck and benefits.

While working as a teacher, Dottie began to write songs and perform them. It was just a hobby, but it kept her dream alive. Then, in the late 1980s, Dottie made a decision. She would retire from teaching and pursue a new career as a performer. In the summer of 1988, she submitted her resignation. Then the terror really hit her. She was so scared

> *The only way to escape from the prison of fear is action.*
>
> — Joe Tye

about venturing into the unknown that she withdrew her resignation and went back to teaching.

But something inside Dottie wouldn't let her dream die. Six months later, in January of 1989, she confronted her fear and retired. At the time, Dottie was in her 50s! In 1992, Dottie developed and performed her own one-woman musical show. The show was based on her fears of leaving a secure teaching job to go into show business!

And in the spring of 1998, Dottie, now in her 60s, released her marvelous CD, *I'm in Love With My Computer*, a collection of witty, inspirational songs. She also performed these songs in a musical revue in a cabaret in New York City — and continues to present her programs of original songs and stories in theaters and cabarets... as well as for organizations throughout the country.

Dottie will be the first to admit that her career transition has been filled with challenges and setbacks. But has it been worth it? According to Dottie, "I've never been happier in my life."

Bravo, Dottie, for confronting your fears... and inspiring us to follow our dreams!

Just Do It

Ralph Waldo Emerson offered some simple advice, which, if followed, can transform your life. He said, *"Do the thing you fear and the death of fear is certain."* I know this advice makes good sense, but some people are just too afraid to act. Remember my prior words about the steep price you pay when you let your fears dominate you.

In the end, running away from your fears is a losing strategy. It will only bring you frustration and unhappiness. I can tell you that from personal experience.

> *Running away from your fears is a losing strategy.*
> — *Jeff Keller*

There's nothing wrong with having some fears. Successful people have fears. The difference is that successful people take action and move forward despite being afraid. It's not always easy, I'll grant that. But you'll always feel better about yourself when you face your fears.

In the last 20 years or so, I've had the privilege of traveling throughout the United States and abroad... and of speaking with thousands of people. During all this time, I haven't met one person who confronted his or her fears... took action... and later regretted it. Not a single one! But I've met *many* people who tell me how much they regret backing away from their fears — and letting their dreams die.

As my friend Burke Hedges often says, *"Don't be one of those who lets his regrets take the place of his dreams."*

So, stretch yourself. Confront your fears and be willing to expand your comfort zone. The courage muscle can be developed just like any other muscle — with exercise. And when you do an activity outside your comfort zone a few times, you know what happens? That same activity becomes part of your comfort zone!

There's another bonus when you're willing to expand your comfort zone. When you push through fear and take action in some areas of your life, you'll develop confidence in other areas, as well. It's true! As I became more comfortable as a speaker, I also became a better salesman... a better businessman... a better listener... the list goes on and on.

You can try to dance around it all you want. But you won't develop your abilities to the fullest unless you're willing to be uncomfortable. Life doesn't reward those who refuse to expose themselves to difficulties and challenges. It's important that you put yourself in a position to win — and that means taking action despite fear.

Confront your fears... and you're on the way to developing your potential and leading the exciting, fulfilling life you deserve. It's a decision you'll never regret!

Get Out There
and Fail

*Failure is only the opportunity to more intelligently
begin again.*

— Henry Ford

*S*he couldn't pay her credit card bills for 26 years.
She moved 25 times looking for work.
She was fired 18 times.
*She worked for 26 years before she earned an annual salary of
$22,000.*
She occasionally lived on food stamps and slept in her car.

You're probably thinking, "If this is a book about success, why are you droning on and on about a woman who had so many failures?"

I'll tell you why. The "failure" described above is well-known TV talk show host Sally Jessy Raphael. You see, despite all of her setbacks, she refused to give up her childhood dream of a career in broadcasting.

She was willing to keep failing... and keep failing... until she succeeded. Sally Jessy Raphael has earned millions of dollars and enjoyed a long and successful TV career. All because she kept a great attitude despite years of failures.

In The Beginning

How is it that someone like Sally Jessy Raphael can endure 26 years of failure and keep going? If you look back to your own childhood, I think you'll see that you, too, demonstrated tremendous resilience in the face of repeated failures.

Remember when you learned how to ride a bicycle? You probably began with training wheels. Eventually, when these crutches were removed, keeping your balance became more difficult. You struggled to stay upright, maybe even falling a few times and scraping yourself. You were learning an important early lesson about failure.

As you practiced, it's likely that one of your parents walked beside you shouting instructions, encouraging you and catching you as you lost balance. You were scared... but excited! You looked forward to the time when you would succeed, when you would at last ride free on your own. So you kept at it every day, and eventually mastered the skill of riding a bike.

What contributed to your ultimate success in learning how to ride your bike? Well, *persistence* and sheer *repetition*, certainly. You were going to stick with it no matter how long it took! It also helped that you were *enthusiastic* about what you set out to achieve — that you could hardly wait to reach your goal. And finally, let's not underestimate the impact of positive *encouragement*. You always knew your parents were in your corner, supporting you, rooting for your success.

As a six-year-old learning to ride your bike, you were optimistic... thrilled... and eager to meet the challenge. You couldn't wait to try again. You knew you'd master it eventually.

But that was a long time ago.

Yesterday And Today

Now let's examine how most adults approach the development of new skills. Would you say they're optimistic...

thrilled... and eager to meet the challenge? We both know the answer to that question is "NO."

Let's assume we asked a group of adults to learn a new software program or to switch to another position in the company. How would most respond?

They'd try to avoid it.

They'd complain.

They'd make excuses why they shouldn't have to do it.

They'd doubt their abilities.

They'd be afraid.

What happened to that six-year-old brimming with vitality and a sense of adventure? How did that child turn into an adult moaning and groaning about learning something new? As adults, most of us become *a lot* more concerned about the opinions of others, often hesitating because people may laugh at us or criticize us.

At the age of six, we knew we had to fall off the bike and get back on to learn a new skill. Falling off the bike wasn't a "bad" thing. But as we got older, we started to perceive falling off as a bad thing — rather than an essential part of the process of achieving our goal.

> *Success is going from failure to failure without loss of enthusiasm.*
> — Winston Churchill

As I pointed out in Lesson 10, it can be uncomfortable to try something new, perhaps even scary. But if you take your eyes off the goal and instead focus your attention on how others may be viewing you, you're doing yourself a grave disservice. To develop a new skill or reach a meaningful target, you must be committed to doing what it takes to get there, even if it means putting up with negative feedback or falling on your face now and then.

Successful people have learned to "fail" their way to success. While they may not particularly *enjoy* their "failures," they recognize them as a *necessary* part of the road to victory. After all, becoming proficient at any skill requires time, effort and discipline... and the willingness to persevere through whatever difficulties may arise.

These Failures Make Millions of Dollars

Take the example of a professional baseball player. As it is today, the player who gets just *three hits in 10 attempts* is at the *top* of his profession, making several million dollars a year. That's a 70 percent failure rate! And the fans will no doubt taunt him when he strikes out.

And speaking of baseball, there's nothing more exciting than watching a player hit a home run. Hank Aaron is the current home run leader with 755 home runs. What you may not know is that he struck out 1,383 times in his career. That's right. Hank had almost twice as many strikeouts as home runs. Yet people remember Hank Aaron for the balls he hit over the wall and not for the pitches he missed.

> *The greatest mistake a person can make is to be afraid of making one.*
> — Elbert Hubbard

When I ask you to name the best basketball player of all time, who comes to mind? I'm guessing that many of you immediately thought of Michael Jordan. He gets my vote. Let me share with you this statistic — Michael Jordan has a career shooting percentage of 50 percent. In other words, half of the shots he took in his career were "failures."

Of course, this principle isn't limited to sports. We also know that show business stars and media personalities are no strangers to failure. Many actors invest 10 or 15 years, enduring *hundreds* of rejections before landing a part that launches their careers. And then, even after achieving some degree of success, they still experience occasional box office flops.

On the night he graduated from college, Jerry Seinfeld did his first comedy gig. It was at a comedy club in New York City. He bombed. When asked to describe that evening, Seinfeld said, "It was pretty horrible. It was a terrible sinking feeling." But he didn't quit. He kept performing his stand-up routine at night. He had five very tough years. And then he was invited to appear on *The Tonight Show* with

Johnny Carson in 1981. He was a big hit... and on his way to an incredibly successful career.

In a nutshell, all these individuals realize that success, to a large extent, is a matter of persistence. That is, if you keep trying, keep developing yourself and keep making adjustments along the way, you're *going* to succeed. You simply need to get enough at-bats... go on enough auditions... visit enough potential clients.

Undaunted By Failure

I want to tell you about two guys who wrote a book containing a collection of inspirational stories. They figured it would take about three months to make a deal with a publisher.

The first publisher they approached said "NO."

The second publisher said "NO."

The third publisher said "NO."

The next 30 publishers said "NO."

Having racked up 33 rejections over a period of three years, what do you think they did? They submitted their book to another publisher.

The 34th publisher said "YES."

And that one "YES" — after 33 "failures" — is what launched the spectacular success of *Chicken Soup For The Soul*, written and compiled by Jack Canfield and Mark Victor Hansen. If you've been in a bookstore in the last 10 years, I'll bet you've seen that book. There's a good chance that you've read one of the books in the *Chicken Soup* series.

The *Chicken Soup For The Soul* series has sold over 100 million copies! All because Jack Canfield and Mark Victor Hansen had the determination to fail over and over... and to keep going until they succeeded.

What sustained Jack Canfield and Mark Victor Hansen through 33 failures? Their attitudes! If these guys had negative attitudes, they would have given up after the first or second rejection, missing out on a pot of gold. But their attitudes remained positive and upbeat — failure... after failure... after failure.

What's a good attitude worth? In their case, about tens of millions of dollars... and still counting!

No Overnight Success

Another example of someone who endured years of failure is movie star Harrison Ford. In the mid-1960s, Ford sought acting jobs. He had little early success and was told by film executives that he lacked "star quality." When Ford had trouble supporting his family, he gave up acting and worked as a carpenter. He was introduced to George Lucas, who gave him a part in the 1973 movie, *American Graffiti*. A few years later, Lucas cast him as Han Solo in *Star Wars*, and Ford was on his way to super-stardom.

> *Success seems to be largely a matter of hanging on after others have let go.*
>
> — William Feather

So, when you get right down to it, *there is no such thing as "failure"* — there are only results, some more successful than others. Failure doesn't mean you've reached the end of the line and that success isn't possible. The only time success is impossible is when you quit. Quitting is final. But continued attempts, with commitment and diligence, can be turned into success.

Never Give Up

In the early 1990s, the owner of a midwestern company called our office to inquire about my speaking programs, as well as our products and publications. I spoke with him on the phone and promptly sent out some information. When we called to follow up, he'd say that he was "thinking about it and hadn't made a decision yet."

At the beginning, we called every week. No sale. Then, we called once a month. No sale. For a period of a few *years*, we kept calling this gentleman. We kept sending him quarterly newsletters and flyers. And all we had to show for it was one failure after another.

But in the spring of 1998, a representative of his company called our office, and I was hired to present a motivational program at one of their sales meetings. When I met the owner in person, he told me, "I was impressed with your persistence. Someone from your office kept calling me for years... and didn't give up."

Sure, we put up with years of failure. But it was all worth it when we made that sale!

Key Questions

If you aren't getting the results you want or have been discouraged by failures, ask yourself these questions:

1. *Do I have an unrealistic timetable?* Maybe you expect to "skip steps" and succeed on a grand scale immediately. Success is usually achieved by climbing one step at a time. And you don't always know how long it will take to advance to the next level. So, be patient with yourself — and resist the temptation to compare your progress with that of anyone else! You'll advance faster than some, slower than others. Maintain a great attitude... take action... make adjustments... and the results will come.

2. *Am I truly committed?* Do you have a burning desire to achieve your goal? It's essential that you be willing to do *whatever it takes* and that you banish any thought of giving up before you accomplish your objective. Of course, it's much easier to be committed when you *love* what you're doing. Therefore, go after those goals you're passionate about, and harbor no thought of quitting.

3. *Do I have too many discouraging influences?* Unsuccessful results can be frustrating. That's why we need to surround ourselves with people who support and believe in us. If you hang around with negative people who are highly critical or who are doing very little in their own lives, your energy and enthusiasm will be

drained. Therefore, develop a network of individuals to encourage and coach you toward success.

4. *Am I preparing to succeed?* Success in any endeavor requires thorough preparation. Are you taking steps to learn everything you can about accomplishing your goal? This means reading books, taking courses and networking with highly successful people in your field. It might mean finding a mentor or getting a coach to work with you. Successful individuals are *always* sharpening their skills. Those getting unsuccessful outcomes often do the same things over and over without making necessary adjustments. So, be "coachable." Accept the fact that you don't already know it all and find resources to keep you on track and moving forward.

> *Would you like me to give you a formula for success? It's quite simple. Double your rate of failure.*
>
> — Thomas J. Watson

5. *Am I truly willing to fail?* Face it, failure is inevitable. You *will* encounter defeat prior to succeeding. In our hearts, we know our most valuable lessons come from our failures. Failure is essential for growth. Look failure squarely in the face and see it as a natural part of the success process. Then, failure will lose its power over you. The truth is, when you're not afraid to fail, you're well on the way to success. Welcome failure as an unavoidable yet vital component in the quest to achieve your goals.

Turning Failure Into Success

Your failures are learning experiences that point out the adjustments you must make. *Never* try to hide from failure, for that approach guarantees that you'll take virtually no risks... and achieve very little. As Beverly Sills once remarked, "*You may be disappointed if you fail, but you are doomed if you don't try."*

No, you won't close *every* sale. And you won't make money on *every* investment. Life is a series of wins and losses, even for the most successful. The winners in life know that you crawl before you walk and you walk before you run. And with each new goal comes a new set of failures. It's up to you whether you treat these disappointments as temporary setbacks and challenges to overcome, or as insurmountable obstacles.

If you make it your business to learn from every defeat and stay focused on the end result you wish to attain, failure will eventually lead you to success!

Networking That Gets Results

*You can get everything in life you want if you'll just
help enough other people get what they want.*
— Zig Ziglar

W hen I met freelance copywriter Stu Kamen in the fall
of 1990, it set off an incredible chain reaction that would
forever impact my business. Let me share with you what
happened.

In 1992, Stu was a contributing writer with *Think & Grow
Rich* newsletter. At Stu's suggestion, that newsletter ran a
front page story about me — and how I went from being a
lawyer to a motivational speaker. At the same time, I entered
into an agreement with that newsletter where they would
sell my "Attitude is Everything" merchandise through their
publication. Thousands of items were sold.

Think & Grow Rich newsletter also began to run some
of my own articles in their publication. As a result, I got
calls from their readers and was hired for several speaking
engagements.

I also got a letter from one of their subscribers named Jim Donovan, who lived in New York at that time. We became good friends. Jim referred me to INTI Publishing & Resource Books, the publisher of the book you're now holding in your hand. By the way, Jim went on to write two great self-help books of his own — *Handbook To A Happier Life* and *This Is Your Life, Not A Dress Rehearsal.*

> *If you're positive and enthusiastic, people will want to spend time with you.*
>
> — Jeff Keller

And all of these great things happened because I tapped into Stu Kamen's network... and then the *Think & Grow Rich* newsletter's network... and then Jim Donovan's network. The power of networking is nothing short of awesome!

If given the choice, wouldn't you like to succeed sooner rather than later? Well, networking is a way to leverage your own efforts and accelerate the pace at which you get results. After all, the more solid relationships you build, the greater your opportunities for success.

The Benefits Of Networking

While your success certainly *starts* with you, it grows to higher levels as a result of your associations and relationships with people. Simply put, you can't succeed on a grand scale all by yourself.

That's why *networking* is so important. For the purposes of this lesson, let's define networking as *the development of relationships with people for mutual benefit.*

In the business arena, networking has the following benefits:

- generates new clients or business leads
- increases employment opportunities
- helps in finding the right people to fill critical positions
- provides valuable information and resources
- assists in solving problems

In the personal realm, here's what networking can do for you:
- enhance your social relationships by introducing you to new friends
- help you to become acquainted with people of varying ethnic, cultural and philosophical backgrounds
- provide valuable information and resources
- contribute to your spiritual growth

Now that we know what networking can do, the question is: What can we do to enhance the effectiveness of our network? Let me pass along 16 techniques that I've found productive. To simplify matters, I've organized them into four separate, but related, categories: 1) attitude and action; 2) referrals; 3) communication; and 4) follow-up.

ATTITUDE AND ACTION

1. *Project a winning attitude.* When it comes to networking, *attitude is everything!* If you're positive and enthusiastic, people will want to spend time with you. They'll want to help you. If you're gloomy and negative, people will avoid you, and they'll hesitate to refer you to their friends and colleagues.

2. *Participate actively in groups and organizations.* Effective networking and relationship-building takes more than paying dues, putting your name in a directory and showing up for meetings. You must demonstrate that you'll take the time and make the effort to contribute to the group.

   What kinds of things can you do? For starters, you can volunteer for committees or serve as an officer or member of the board of directors. The other members will respect you when they see you roll up your sleeves and do some work. They'll also learn about your people skills, your character, your values and last, but not least, your attitude!

Let's get back to Stu Kamen for a moment. He wanted to build contacts within advertising agencies, so he joined the Long Island Advertising Club in 1994. Stu immediately began to attend the group's meetings. When they asked for volunteers for various projects, Stu raised his hand. He got *actively* involved!

Within six months after joining, somebody approached him and said, "We hear good things about you. You're a hard worker and very energetic. Would you like to join our board of directors?" As you might guess, Stu gladly accepted. And within a few months, he began to see a significant increase in his business. In early 1999, Stu told me that well over 50 percent of his current business can be traced to people he met through the Long Island Advertising Club — proving that people can get big results in a short time by networking effectively.

3. *SERVE OTHERS in your network.* Serving others is crucial to building and benefiting from your network! You should *always* be thinking, "How can I serve others?" instead of "What's in it for me?" If you come across as desperate or as a "taker" rather than a "giver," you won't find people willing to help you. Going the extra mile for others is the best way to get the flow of good things coming back to you.

Getters don't get —
givers get.

— Eugene Benge

How can you serve others in your network? Start by referring business leads or potential customers. In addition, whenever you see an article or other information that might be of interest to someone in your network, forward the material to that person.

When I think of effective networkers, the first name that comes to mind is Mark LeBlanc. Mark gives presentations to business owners who want to grow their business and to salespeople who want to sell more of their products and services. I've referred many people to Mark. Why? He's a talented, service-oriented person who has gone out of his way to encourage me... and to help me build my business.

Mark has put me in touch with people in his own network who are in a position to help me. He distributes my materials at his presentations. Mark is one of those people who just keeps giving... and giving... and giving. That's why people want to help Mark — and that's one reason why his own business is growing!

As the Bible says, "Give and it shall be given unto you." That's the truth!

REFERRALS

4. *If you refer someone, make sure that the person mentions your name as the source of the referral.* Be explicit. Let's assume you're about to refer John Smith to your graphic designer, Jane Jones. You might say to John, "Give Jane a call, and please tell her that I referred you." In some instances, you may even call Jane and let her know that John Smith will be contacting her.

Then, the next time you see or speak to Jane, remember to ask if John called and how it turned out. You want to reinforce in Jane's mind that you're looking out for her and helping her to grow her business.

5. *Be selective. Don't refer every person you meet.* Respect the time of those in your network. Referring "unqualified" leads will reflect poorly on *you*. Ask yourself whether or not a particular referral is *really* going to be of value to your network partner. Keep in mind that the key is the *quality*, not quantity, of the leads you supply.

COMMUNICATION

6. *Be a good listener.* Have you ever been speaking to someone who goes on and on about himself and his

business — and never takes a moment to ask about you? We've all run into the "Me, Me, Me" types — and they're the last people you want to help.

So, in your conversations, focus on drawing other people out. Let them talk about their careers and interests. In return, you'll be perceived as caring, concerned and intelligent. You'll eventually get your turn to talk about yourself. Sure, this is Dale Carnegie 101... but it works!

7. *Call people from time to time just because you care.* How do you feel when someone calls you on the phone and says, "Hey, I was just thinking about you and was wondering how you're doing?" I'll bet you feel like a million bucks! If that's the case, why don't we make these calls more often?

> *You can succeed best and quickest by helping others to succeed.*
>
> — Napoleon Hill

Every now and then, make it a point to call people in your network simply to ask how they're doing and to offer your support and encouragement. That's right. Call just because you care — and because that's the way you'd like to be treated.

Every December, I pick up the phone and call certain clients I haven't spoken with for a long time. Many of these people haven't ordered anything from my company in years. My call is upbeat and my only agenda is to be friendly. I don't try to sell them anything. I appreciate the business they've given me in the past, and I just want to hear how they're doing, personally and professionally.

If business comes from these calls, that's great.

If business doesn't come from these calls, that's great.

Year after year, I do get business as a result of making these calls. Someone will say, "I need to order more of those *Attitude is Everything* lapel pins" or "Our company is having a sales meeting in six months, and they may want you to do a presentation."

Please understand that this isn't manipulation or a sales tactic on my part. I'm not expecting these people to give me business. I really care about how they're doing. Business is simply a by-product of re-connecting with them.

8. *Take advantage of everyday opportunities to meet people.* You can make excellent contacts just about anywhere — at the health club or on line at the supermarket. You never know from what seed your next valuable relationship will sprout.

When I go to the gym on the weekends, I always wear an "Attitude is Everything" shirt. It's a great icebreaker and people will come up to me to talk about attitude. It gives me an opportunity to learn about them — and to tell them about my company.

9. *Treat every person as important — not just the "influential" ones.* Don't be a snob. The person you meet (whether or not they're *the boss*) may have a friend or relative who can benefit from your product or service. So, when speaking to someone at a meeting or party, give that person your undivided attention.

And please promise me that you won't be one of those who gazes around looking for "more important people" to talk to. That really bugs me. You're talking with someone and then he notices someone out of the corner of his eye — someone he deems more important than you! So he stops listening to you... and abruptly breaks away to start a conversation with that other person. Don't do that! Treat every person you encounter with dignity and respect.

10. *At meetings and seminars, make it a point to meet different people.* Don't sit with the same group at every

gathering. While it's great to talk with friends for part of the meeting, you'll reap greater benefits if you make the extra effort to meet new faces.

In 1994, I was in Washington, D.C., to attend the annual convention of the National Speakers Association. At lunch, instead of sitting with some friends, I sat down at a table where I didn't know anyone. Sitting at that table was a woman named Joan Burge — and we struck up a conversation. Her company, Office Dynamics, conducts excellent training programs for administrative office professionals.

It turned out that Joan is also a big believer that attitude is everything! And, nearly 15 years later, she still orders my "Attitude is Everything" lapel pins and distributes them to some of the participants in her training programs. In addition, Joan often displays my literature at her programs, which has generated thousands of dollars in business for me. Most importantly, Joan has become a wonderful friend.

I'm sure glad I didn't sit with my friends that day, as I would have missed out on a tremendous opportunity!

11. *Be willing to go beyond your comfort zone.* For instance, if you have the urge to introduce yourself to someone, DO IT! You might hesitate, thinking that the person is too important or too busy to speak with you. Even if you're nervous, force yourself to move forward and make contact. You'll get more comfortable as time goes on.

12. *Ask for what you want.* By helping others, you've now earned the right to request assistance yourself. Don't be shy. As long as you've done your best to serve those in your network, they'll be more than willing to return the favor.

FOLLOW-UP

13. *Send a prompt note after meeting someone for the first time.* Let's say you attend a dinner and make a new contact. Send a short note as soon as possible explaining how much you enjoyed meeting and talking with him or her. Enclose some of your own materials and perhaps include information that might be of interest to this person (such as the name of a trade magazine and a subscription card). Ask if there's anything you can do to assist this individual.

> *Treat every person you encounter with dignity and respect.*
> — Jeff Keller

   Be sure to send the note *within 48 hours* after your initial meeting so that it's received while you're still fresh in your contact's mind.

14. *Acknowledge powerful presentations or articles.* If you hear an interesting presentation or read a great article, send a note to the speaker or writer and tell him or her how much you enjoyed and learned from their message. One person in a hundred will take the time to do this — be the one who does!

   I'm not saying that speakers and writers are special people who deserve to be worshipped. The point is, speakers and writers often have developed a huge network of people covering a variety of industries — a network you can tap into!

15. *When you receive a referral or helpful written materials, ALWAYS send a thank you note or call to express your appreciation.* Follow this suggestion only if you want to receive more referrals and more useful information. If you don't acknowledge that person sufficiently, he or she will be much less likely to assist you in the future.

16. *Send congratulatory cards and letters.* If someone in your network gets a promotion, award or celebrates some other occasion (for example, a marriage or birth of a child) write a short note of congratulations. Everyone loves to be recognized, yet very few people take the time to do this. Being thoughtful in this manner can only make you stand out. It's also appropriate to send a card or memorial gift when a family member dies.

Building Your Network

The networking suggestions offered above are merely the tip of the iceberg. You should be able to come up with several new ideas of your own. How? By going to your library or bookstore and seeking out the many excellent books on networking… and by noticing what other people are doing and adapting their ideas in a way that suits you.

Remember that networks are built over time and that significant results usually don't show up immediately. So be patient! Build a solid foundation of relationships and continue to expand and strengthen them. You'll have to put in a lot before you begin reaping the big rewards.

One final point: Great networking skills are not a substitute for being excellent in your field. You might be a terrific PR person, but if you aren't talented at what you do — and constantly learning and improving — your efforts will yield disappointing results.

Now, go ahead! Select a few of these networking techniques and implement them right away. Get to work serving and improving your network. Then you will truly have an army of troops working to help you succeed!

CONCLUSION ─────────

Change Your Attitude and You Change Your Life

> *To change your circumstances, first start thinking differently.*
> — Norman Vincent Peale

July 28, 2006. Atlanta, Georgia
  I just finished giving a presentation in a large ballroom to hundreds of people who had come to Atlanta for a weekend seminar that featured some of the best speakers in the self-development field, including Jim Rohn and Bob Proctor. As you may know, Jim Rohn and Bob Proctor are "legends" in the self-help industry. Each has spoken to millions of people worldwide over a span of 40-plus years.

  When everyone left the room, I was about to gather up all my things. But for some reason, I paused for a moment. I flashed back to 1985, when I sat in my den, negative and depressed. At that time, I had just started listening to audio programs by Jim Rohn and Bob Proctor. Now, more than 20 years later, I had the honor of speaking on the same stage with them!

"How did this happen?" I thought to myself.

The answer came to me loud and clear. *I changed my attitude.*

You see, when you change your attitude, sparks fly in the universe. You're energized. You begin to see new possibilities. You move into action. You achieve extraordinary results. That's why I say *when you change your attitude, you change your life!*

Now I'd be kidding you if I told you the last 20 years were just a string of successes. Far from it. I've had my share of defeats and setbacks along the way. But the success principles I've discussed in this book are what have given me the courage, the guidance and the strength to keep moving forward.

Take Control Of Your Life

I applaud you for taking the time to read this book. It shows that you're truly interested in developing your incredible potential. Yet, reading this book is only the first step to living the life you want to live. When you focus on these ideas — and take action to implement them — you're on the way to creating some exciting breakthroughs in your life.

Act as if it were impossible to fail.
— Dorothea Brande

You may have seen statistics that only about five percent of the population reaches a high level of success. Why is that? After 20 years of research, I'm convinced it comes down to this:

It's the *rare individual* who applies the success principles discussed in this book on a *daily* basis.

It's the rare individual who consistently maintains a positive attitude, knowing that his thoughts will become his reality.

It's the rare individual who watches the words he uses, knowing that he's programming his mind for success, mediocrity or failure.

It's the rare individual who has the guts to confront her fears, because that's where her potential will be developed — by doing things she's afraid to do.

It's the rare individual who looks for the silver lining in every dark cloud.

And it's the rare individual who makes a commitment, follows through with a positive attitude... and has the persistence to get the job done.

I challenge you to be one of those rare individuals.

You have the potential to become more than you ever dreamed. You have greatness within you... and your attitude is the key to unlocking that potential. Changing my attitude changed my life. And if a better attitude can work miracles in my life, it can work miracles in yours!

I'd like to share with you these words from Dr. Charles Swindoll, who captured the essence of attitude — and how it dominates the direction of our lives:

"The longer I live, the more I realize the impact of attitude on life. Attitude, to me, is more important than facts. It is more important than the past, than education, than money, than circumstances, than failures, than successes, than what other people think or say or do. It is more important than appearance, giftedness or skill. It will make or break a company... a church... a home.

"The remarkable thing is we have a choice every day regarding the attitude we will embrace for that day. We cannot change our past... we cannot change the fact that people will act in a certain way. We cannot change the inevitable. The only thing we can do is play on the one string we have, and that is our attitude.

"I am convinced that life is 10 percent what happens to me and 90 percent how I react to it. And so it is with you... we are in charge of our Attitudes."

Pretty powerful words, aren't they? Do what Charles Swindoll suggests and "play on the one string you have" — your ATTITUDE.

Now is the time to take control of your attitude. Now is the time to start creating miracles in your own life.

Go ahead — believe in yourself. Have the courage and persistence to follow your dreams. And above all, never, never forget that... *Attitude is Everything!*

May God bless you on your journey.